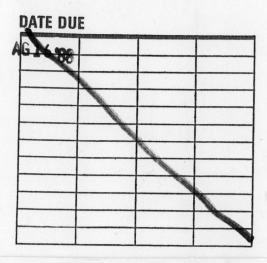

Coleen Kent Menlove earned her master's degree in education
from Brigham Young University, Provo, Utah.
After several years teaching experience in public schools,
Coleen, the mother of six children, is now giving
"Ready, Set, Go!" workshops to parent groups
within the community

Coleen Kent Menlove

ready, set, go!

give your children
a head start before they go to school

**Illustrations by
Ja Neanne A. Webster**

A SPECTRUM BOOK

PRENTICE-HALL, INC., *Englewood Cliffs, New Jersey 07632*

Library of Congress Cataloging in Publication Data

MENLOVE, COLEEN KENT.
   Ready, set, go!

   (A Spectrum book)
   Bibliography: p.
   Includes index.
     1. Domestic education.   2. Education, Preschool.
I. Title.
LC37.M46   372.21   78-9640
ISBN 0-13-762286-4
ISBN 0-13-762278-3 pbk.

© 1978 by Prentice-Hall, Inc.,
Englewood Cliffs, N.J. 07632

A SPECTRUM BOOK

Printed in the United States of America

10 9 8 7 6 5 4 3 2 1

PRENTICE-HALL INTERNATIONAL, INC., *London*
PRENTICE-HALL OF ASTRALIA PTY. LIMITED, *Sydney*
PRENTICE-HALL OF CANADA, LTD., *Toronto*
PRENTICE-HALL OF INDIA PRIVATE LIMITED, *New Delhi*
PRENTICE-HALL OF JAPAN, INC., *Tokyo*
PRENTICE-HALL OF SOUTHEAST ASIA PTE. LTD., *Singapore*
WHITEHALL BOOKS LIMITED, *Wellington, New Zealand*

preface

Since the beginning of time, mothers have sought to provide their young children with a variety of pleasurable play experiences, if for no other reason than that an occupied child is a happy, satisfied child. However, in recent years mothers have become increasingly aware of the importance of play in training and in teaching the child to meet the demands of the world more successfully.

The Head Start program and others like it awakened a realization of the importance of the play opportunities that are provided in the home environment. Research has clearly indicated that a rich home environment providing a variety of firsthand play experiences can have a great impact on the child's potential learning ability.

In recent years several books have been published containing mountains of theoretical advice to parents, and a few of these books contain a scant list of ideas for activities for the child. As parents have become familiar with the basic principles of enriching the child's environment, they have expressed a need for more practical how-to ideas. This book contains a short review of the child-development principles involved in teaching skills to the young child, and an extensive collection of firsthand, skill-oriented activities that can be administered to the young child in the home with basic materials.

It is the author's hope that such firsthand, experience-oriented activities will provide parents with the necessary ideas to give their children the essential ingredients for optimal development and enable the child to successfully meet the challenges of formal education.

It has been found also that through these activities parents and child can find a new closeness and understanding of each other. The parents find that being a teaching parent can be fun and rewarding, and the child discovers that the parents really care—enough to step into the life of the child and be a part of his world. This last discovery may prove to be of more benefit to the parents and child than teaching the child skills through first-hand experiences.

credits

Acknowledgment and appreciation is given to the mothers who participated in testing the ideas and activities found in this program and for their efforts and enthusiasm during the trial period.

Gratitude is also expressed to the Menlove children — Drew, Chad, Mindi, Mitch, Margaret, and Marc — who were the inspiration for the development of the program.

A special word of thanks and appreciation is expressed to the author's husband Dean, whose encouragement and support throughout the project made its completion possible.

COMMENTS FROM MOTHERS
WHO HAVE USED THE PROGRAM

A lot of exciting things to do with real-life objects—excellent variety!

I loved it. I have been wanting just such a plan to guide me in my activities with my child.

I feel that it really is helping us to understand and communicate with each other. My child realizes more that I care for him.

He wondered what was with me trying so many new things that I hadn't taken time to do before.

I was able to minimize conflicts or moments of boredom by suggesting some new and interesting activities. I sometimes used the program to relieve cold-war tension!

I liked the organization of the activities. I could gear the level of the activities up or down to the level of my child.

It truly opens my horizons, if not the child's.

The program helped me tremendously in teaching my daughter. It helped me realize some of her strong and weak points.

It was fun for the whole family.

I was amazed at how many activities I had overlooked or hadn't thought of.

Many of the activities I already did with my boy, but did not realize the value of what they were teaching. It helped make me aware of how I can make daily activities teaching experiences.

contents

ready

introduction 1

there is, as never before in the history of America, an increasing emphasis on the education of the young child. Educators and government leaders are realizing the importance of enriching the experiences of the young child to prepare him more adequately for the experiences of school life. Many preschool children learn "with sponge-like absorption."[1] During these first few formative years, much can be done to interest and inspire the child and to whet his curiosity for learning about the world around him.[2]

The future belongs to the young child. We have the task of helping him develop. We cannot sit idly by and hope that he will flower, because he will not. We have to find and define the optimum environment for the young child and then provide it for him.[3]

WHERE AND HOW TO EDUCATE THE YOUNG CHILD

This recognition of the importance of early experience in relationship to intelligence and learning has been facilitated by an increasing number of studies. Research attests to the view that the development of both general and specific cognitive abilities — the abilities required for success in school — are determined in many critical ways by the availability of relevant experiences in the preschool environment.

Bloom estimated that the effect of living in a "culturally deprived" as against a "culturally abundant" environment to be 20 IQ points, and he hypothesizes that this effect is spaced devel-

[1]Para Porter, *Practical Ideas and Activities for Pre-School Enrichment Programs* (Wolfe City, Texas: Henington Publishing Co., 1966), p. 5.
[2]Ibid.
[3]Ira Gordon, speech delivered at the conference on The Young Child: Florida's Future, at the University of Florida, June 16, 1967.

opmentally, so that the years from birth to four years show a loss of 10 of those 20 IQ points.[4] Not only does research underscore the importance of a culturally abundant environment, consisting of a variety of firsthand experiences, in development of a child's potential, but research further indicates that the best place for that education is in the home under the direction of loving parents.

Milner found a significant relationship between the reading readiness of first-grade children and the "verbal environment" at home.[5] Hess has found the same relationship for the acquisition of language and the nature of the mother-child interaction.[6] Thus it becomes clear that education of parents as to the basic first-hand activities they can provide for the child is the best approach in providing an optimal environment to give the young child the essential ingredients for optimal development.

PARENTS CAN BE TEACHERS

There are some specialists who urge parents to stop trying to teach their young children in order that the children may learn. There is something to be said for this statement; it is all too easy for planned learning experiences to become didactic and regimented, rather than subtle and spontaneous. But can parents expect that all the necessary learning experience will occur without formal planning?

There is an old legend that if you put six chimpanzees in front of six typewriters and leave them there long enough, they eventually will produce all the literary works in the British Museum. One could paraphrase this for early childhood by suggesting that

[4]Benjamin S. Bloom, *Stability and Change in Human Characteristics,* (New York: John Wiley & Sons, Inc., 1964).

[5]Esther Milner, A Study of the Relationship Between Reading Readiness in Grade One School Children and Patterns of Parent-Child Interactions. *Child Development,* 22, 1951, pp. 95–122.

[6]Robert D. Hess, "Inventory of Compensatory Education Projects," (Chicago, Illinois: School of Education, University of Chicago), mimeographed, 1965.

six children with good eyes and ears and hands and brains would, if left alone in nature, arrive at a number system, discover the laws of conservation of matter and energy, comprehend gravity and motion of the planets, and perhaps arrive at the theory of relativity. All the circumstances necessary to discern these relationships are readily available. Perhaps a more realistic example would be this: If we surrounded a group of young children with a carefully selected set of play materials, they would eventually discover for themselves the laws of color mixture, form and contour, perspective, formal rhythm and tonal relationships, and biological growth. We would also assume that at a still earlier period a child would learn body control, eye-hand coordination, the rudiments of language, and styles of problem solving in an entirely incidental and unplanned way.[7]

To be sure, all this could occur, but the chances of this occurring with any frequency are very unlikely. Would you like to leave your child's learning up to such chances? As more people gain experience with young children, the conviction appears to be gaining momentum that the young child must be guided into meaningful learning encounters.

One of the strongest arguments for the importance of the parents' role in teaching the young child is the concept of modeling. To some degree the research indicates that one way to learn to ride a bike is to first watch other people ride one, see what they are doing, and then try to copy their behavior. Just as painters, pianists, and even professional football players model excellence in their fields of pursuit, children model their activity on their parents' activity. Children desire to imitate, to copy, and to relate to those closest and most important to them — their parents. This is a real key to early learning. Parents are responsible for the inputs they control. Research tells us that the earlier the inputs, the greater the gain. Parents have the opportunity to influence the child's perceptual experiences from the first moment of birth.[8]

[7]Bettye M. Caldwell, "What Is the Optimal Learning Environment for the Young Child?" *American Journal of Orthopsychiatry,* XXXVII (January, 1967), p. 15.

[8]Gordon, speech.

As stated previously the optimal environment for the young child is one in which the child is cared for in his own home in the context of a warm, continuous, emotional relationship with his own parents under conditions of varied sensory input. Implicit in this principle is the conviction that the child's parents are qualified to provide a stable and warm interpersonal relationship as well as the proper learning environment. This places a great responsibility upon parents and assumes that they possess or will quickly acquire all the talents necessary to create an optimal learning environment.[9]

Fully cognizant of the role of mothers in early childhood development, Ira Gordon developed the Florida Parent Education Project, by which mothers are instructed in stimulation exercises for their young children. Such instruction is designed to (a) enhance the development of infants and children and (b) increase the mother's competence and sense of personal worth. One of the hopes in the Florida Parent Education Project is that the mother finds her experience with her child so satisfying to her that she continues to seek her own ways of relating to the child.[10]

Many fathers find constructive play with their preschool child to be most enjoyable; and they, too, are interested in providing learning experiences for their child. Research indicates that fathers who include the child in the ongoing conversation, ask the child questions, and verbally stimulate the child, enhance motivation of the preschooler which in turn positively affects the cognitive functions. Attention from the father produces a positive experience for the child, leading to a desire to explore the environment. This is especially true for boys.[11] Blanchard and Biller (1970) studied the effects of low father availability (less than six

[9]Caldwell, "What Is the Optimal Learning Environment for the Young Child?" p. 10.

[10]Gordon, speech.

[11]Ann S. Epstein and Norma Radin, "Motivational Components Related to Father Behavior and Cognitive Function in Preschoolers," *Child Development,* XXVI, (December, 1975), pp. 831–39.

hours a week) versus high father availability. They found that those in high father availability homes surpass the others on achievement test scores. Rosenberg and Landy (1968) suggest that these cognitive deficits may extend into adulthood.[12]

Many educators feel that the hopes for young children's futures are in the hand of the parents. It is this author's belief that parents can develop the talents necessary and that most parents are willing to do all they can to create for their children the proper developmental environment, to provide the basic essentials of physical, psychological, and cognitive development for their children.

Certainly there are situations and times when parents are so overwhelmed with their own reactions of depression and inadequacy that behavior towards the child is largely determined by the needs of the moment—rather than by any clear plan about how to bring up children and how to train them to engage in the kind of behavior that the parents regard as acceptable or desirable. Life with growing children is hectic even during times of relative calm.[13]

However, the depth of satisfaction and enjoyment of these years for parents and young child is limited only by the parents' resourcefulness and the time and effort they are willing to expend. Parents can use teaching moments to help the young child grow in all aspects of development.

There is no doubt, however, that for parents to guide the child into satisfactory learning experiences, they must arm themselves with a knowledge and understanding of the basic principles of child development. And they must have some ideas about how to translate these principles into meaningful firsthand learning experiences for their child.

[12]E. Mavis Hetherington and Jan L. Deur, "The Effects of Father Absence on Child Development," *Young Children*, XLVI, (March, 1971), pp. 233-48.
[13]Caldwell, "What Is the Optimal Learning Environment for the Young Child?" p. 16.

BASIC PRINCIPLES OF CHILD DEVELOPMENT

Although it is vital that parents be familiar with early childhood development principles, it is not the author's purpose to go into a lengthy discussion of these principles. There are others who have very capably set forth the basic principles involved. (And it is the experience of the author that many parents have involved themselves to some degree in a study of these principles and have acquired a general background in child development.) It is important, however, to have a common understanding of basic principles involved to be effective in selecting and administering activities that conform to these basic principles. Therefore, a few pages have been set aside at the beginning of this book for review of early childhood education principles.

FIRSTHAND EXPERIENCE ACTIVITIES

The following program is organized according to subjects of the curriculum; however, the program is not intended to be subject-oriented. The child is the center of all of the activities: The child's current needs and interests must come first. The organization of the activities should help the parent build and expand upon the child's present-day, firsthand experiences and provide suggestions for further firsthand activities to enrich the child's understanding.

Children vary in their interests and capabilities, so a parent should be selective in using the program. The parent should use only activities that the child shows interest in and, if at any time the activity seems to be too difficult for the child, should simplify the activity or leave it for a future day.

The activities listed in this program are only a few of the many possibilities for broadening the child's horizons. It is hoped that parents will be innovative and add to or improve upon the activities listed here.

HOW TO USE THE PROGRAM

The following are suggestions to you for making effective use of the program:

- Become familiar with the underlying principles of the program by reading the following sections:"Characteristics and Needs of the Young Child," "Learning Theories: How Does the Young Child Learn?" and "Curriculum: What Should the Young Child Learn?"
- Select a curriculum area that interests you and your child.
- Read the introductory information for the curriculum area you select.
- Glance over the activities and check a few that appear to be on your child's learning level.
- Prepare materials needed for the activities you select.
- Present the activity to the child. But be flexible: Do not feel that once the activities are begun that they must be completed or must be completed in a certain manner.
- Use positive reinforcement, and remember to praise the child for his efforts as well as for his accomplishments.
- Develop variations on suggested activities, or think of other activities that meet the specific needs of the child. Be creative, and allow the child to be creative in his responses.
- Try other areas of the curriculum, but do not hesitate to return to favorite activities as often as the child desires.
- Have fun with your child as you help to broaden his horizons.

set

2
characteristics and needs of the young child

each child has characteristics that are similar to those of other children the same age. However, each child also has unique characteristics. It is the similarities that enable a teacher to work with children in a group, but it is the parent who can on a one-to-one basis deal most effectively with the unique differences of his own child. Throughout the administration of this program, you must be careful in gauging the material to the level and interest of the child.

To devise an effective curriculum or program of activities for the child, the parent must be aware of his fundamental needs. The physical needs — eating when hungry, having a drink when thirsty, going to the bathroom as necessary, providing a rhythm of activity and rest, providing one or more physical outlets for emotions — must be met before any learning can take place. An unmet need to develop a healthy personality (by furthering a sense of trust, autonomy, initiative, and conscience) can inhibit the learning process. Other needs that must be met are those of safety, security, belonging, adequacy, self-realization and integrity. If this program is presented in an appropriate manner, the needs of the child should be met more effectively because of exposure to first-hand experiences and because of the supportive relationship of the parents.

The following chart contains some very general characteristics and some special needs of three-, four- and five-year-old children, as stated in Todd and Heffenan.

ASPECTS OF DEVELOPMENT OF PRESCHOOL CHILDREN*

Three-Year-Old	Abilities	Implications
Physical	Balances erect	Falls often
	Alternates feet	Climbs stairs
	Stands on one foot	Learns to hop
	Developing Coordination	Jumps, walks and runs with music; unbuttons buttons; rolls ball, throws underhand; toilets self during day; talks, eats by self

ASPECTS OF DEVELOPMENT *(continued)*

Three-Year-Old	Abilities	Implications
Social	Learning to share	Shares toys; not able to share workspace; brings possessions to share in a community activity
	Sensitive to people	Tries to please and conform; feels sympathetic; likes simple guessing; enjoys dressing up; uses the term "we" more
Emotional	Shows self-control	Rests for ten minutes; waits until it is time; takes turns
	Proud of what he makes	Likes to display his work
	Developing independence	Can be self-motivating; Can leave mother more; Plays by himself
Intellectual	Is attentive to words	Responds to adults suggestions; likes to talk with adults; listens longer to stories; enjoys praise and simple humor
	Compares two objects	Builds a three-block bridge; points out objects in a picture
	Participates in planning	Talks about proposed plans; tries out words dramatically

Special Needs: Needs mother love, guidance in working with others, opportunity to use big muscles

ASPECTS OF DEVELOPMENT *(continued)*

Four-Year-Old	Abilities	Implications
Physical	Climbs easily	Learns to use a fireman's pole
	Actively runs, jumps, hops	Covers more ground
	Has more motor control	Learns to skip; saw; cuts on a line; throws overhand
	Has more coordination	Talks and eats, talks and plays
Social	Continuing sensitivity to people	Quotes parents as authorities; dislikes isolation from group; learns to express sympathy; likes to dress up and play dramatically
	More cooperative	Plays with small group
Emotional	Goes out of bounds	Likes to brag; likes freehand drawing (not coloring books)
	Is learning limits	Likes to go on excursions; runs ahead, but waits on corner; interested in rules; plans ahead with adults; acts silly if tired
Intellectual	Experiments with words	Makes up words and rhymes; likes new words, big ones
	Asks "Why?" and "How?"	Runs a topic to the ground; likes to have explanations
	Likes to imagine	Does much dramatic play; learns to distinguish fact and fancy
	Has fluid thought	Interested in death; changes title of his drawing as he draws

ASPECTS OF DEVELOPMENT *(continued)*

Four-Year-Old	Abilities	Implications
Special Needs:	Needs a listening ear for his constant talking, an opportunity to test himself out in relation to other people and his own physical skills, assurance that he is loved and valued	

Five-Year-Old	Abilities	Implications
Physical	Has more motor control	Able to sit longer
	Crosses street safely	Explores neighborhood; does simple errands
	Has more eye-hand control	Learns to lace shoes; learns to use overhead ladder; learns left from right
Social	Is social	More cooperative play; gets along well in small group; conforms to adult ideas; asks adult help
Emotional	Poised and in control	
	Proud of what he has and does	Likes to save and display his work
	Likes to have rules	Learns what is right to do and say
Intellectual	Interests widen	Recognizes some numbers and letters; interested in the clock and time
	Thinks correctly	Asks "What?" and "How?"; learns his address and telephone number
	Has purpose	Draws what he has in mind at the moment
	Is flexible	Is not concerned with inconsistencies

ASPECTS OF DEVELOPMENT *(continued)*

Five-Year-Old	*Abilities*	*Implications*

Special Needs: Needs encouragement, ample praise, warmth and great patience from adults with wise guidance; Opportunity for plenty of activity, equipment for exercising large muscles; Opportunity to do things for himself, freedom to use and develop his own powers; Opportunity to learn about his world by seeing and doing things

*V. E. Todd and H. Heffernan, *The Years Before School: Guiding Preschool Children* (2nd ed.), (New York: Macmillan Co., 1970), pp. 36–37. Reprinted by permission of the publisher. Copyright © 1970 by Macmillan Publishing Co., Inc.

3
learning theories:
how does the young child learn

most experts believe that a child's learning is a result of heredity, maturation, and experiences. Holt has stated that "children have a style of learning that fits their conditions, which they use naturally and well until we train them out of it."[1] Hildebrand believes that "children must learn, want to learn, and will learn.[2] It is not the purpose of this author to set forth and examine all the various theories about learning, for no single theory can adequately explain the learning process for all children. There are, however, a few basic assumptions that influence and direct the philosophy of this program.

More than 50 years ago a Swiss psychologist named Jean Piaget began to talk about the growth of intelligence, at a time when the common notion was that intelligence was affected only by heredity. Piaget believed that intelligence is also deeply affected by the total environment. He reasoned that ideas grow on ideas and that they are the starting point of learning. Piaget's careful clinical studies and writings about the development of intelligence have given educators all over the world clearer ideas about learning. Piaget's research has contributed strong evidence to support the idea that the quality of experience has profound impact on intellectual growth.[3]

In recent years much research has been carried out on Piagetian theory. Investigators have been curious about the validity of Piaget's ideas and have repeated some of his tests. Elkind[4] and Uzgiris have agreed with Piaget's findings as a result of their systematic replication of Piaget's studies.[5] Other findings of research also agree with Piaget's results.

Piaget's findings have great implications for education. A major goal of education is to guide children toward higher levels

[1]John Holt, *How Children Learn* (New York: Pitman, 1967), foreword.

[2]V. Hildebrand, *Introduction to Early Childhood Education* (New York: Macmillan, 1971), p. 3.

[3]Carole Honstead, "The Development Theory of Jean Piaget" (paper), Oregon State University: 1968.

[4]David Elkind, "The Development of Quantitative Thinking: A Systematic Replication of Piaget's Studies,"*J. Gent. Psychol.*, 1961, 98, pp. 37–46.

[5]Ina C. Uzgiris, Situational Generality of Conservation, *Child Development*, 1964, 35, pp. 831–41.

of learning. In order to build ideas on ideas, then, the teacher-parent must start at the child's present level of thinking. In keeping with the Piagetian theory, Hess and Shipman carry the requirement for an enriched program one step further: The experiences must have a pattern of sequential meaning. In addition, activities must relate to each other and to what the child already knows to be meaningful to him.[6]

Today, as never before, emphasis is being placed on the importance of firsthand experiences for the preschool child. First-hand experiences mean that the child must have his freedom in learning about his world. The child should be able to feel, explore, taste, smell, observe, listen, compare, and classify. The child needs opportunities for social approval, opportunities to have questions answered, and opportunities to imitate appropriate models of behavior. Yet this freedom — these opportunities — must be structured, that is, the child does what he wants within reasonable bounds. Unconditionally accepting the child regardless of his behavior or subordinating oneself to the child is not ideal. The child needs and wants wise guidance.

Wise guidance means recognizing where the child is now in his learning and what steps might follow in order to give him a sequential pattern of meaningful learning experiences. Growth in ability will be irregular. At times the rapidity of the young child's development will astound the parent, and yet there will be periods when the child seems to be at a complete standstill. The child, however, may be using such time to absorb what he has learned or to prepare himself for the next spurt, or he may be just enjoying his sense of mastery of some accomplished task. Many times growth in ability is complicated and involves numerous subtle learnings before the objective is understood and achieved.

Wise guidance recognizes the importance of repetition of an activity to aid the child in feeling the security of having learned a skill. Variation of the same task, with increased complexity,

[6]Robert D. Hess and Virginia Shipman, "Early Blocks to Children's Learning, *Children,* 1965, 12, pp. 189-94.

adds the challenge of expansion. The child will give clues as to when he has absorbed the knowledge or developed the skill and is thus ready to expand upon this learning or move on to something completely new. These clues will be best observed if the parents will not become too eager to jump into the child's learning. Parents need to take time to observe how and what learning is occurring.

Wise guidance includes understanding principles of motivation and using them correctly. The child's motivation for learning is an immediate, stimulating pleasure as a result of personal involvement in activity. The child needs to know that his parents will respond in a positive way to his need for attention and recognition. Encouraging comments about his efforts and accomplishments will motivate the child to expand his participation in the learning process. The child is learning to enjoy learning.

4
curriculum:
what should the young child learn?

tape

What is curriculum? To some, curriculum means a course of study to be followed with great care; to others it refers to what is planned for the child to learn; and to still others it designates what the child actually learns as a result of guided experiences. Many today look upon curriculum as the totality of those learning experiences provided that are essential to the maximum development of the individual as a useful member of society.[1]

Regardless of our definition of curriculum, it is the adult, whether teacher or parent-teacher, who must make it work through his own skill and enthusiasm. Tarney warns that it is vital for adults to be alert to their own responses of lack of them.[2] Adults must be aware that a child learns from adult actions, attitudes, and words; in other words, they serve as a model to the child. "The teacher [parent] may be the spark which sets the child off on many different paths or turns his attention to many new things."[3]

The responsibility of the adult is to understand the tasks involved in any concept of curriculum and to recognize that whatever the approach, the goal is to assure maximum learning and maximum love for learning. In a very literal sense, the adult provides but the child decides what his curriculum will be. The child designs his own curriculum as he selects what he wants to learn. Any program or curriculum might be evaluated upon the standard of how narrow the chasm is between what is planned for the child to learn and what the child actually chooses to learn.[4]

Homes provide a curriculum for the young child whether the parents are aware of it or not, and a good preschool curriculum at home is not a haphazard affair, as it all too often becomes. It must be a result of careful planning based on knowledge of the young child and his developmental needs and interests. Through

[1]Lillian M. Logan, *Teaching the Young Child: Methods of Preschool and Primary Education,* (Boston: Houghton Mifflin Co., 1960), p. 106.

[2]E. D. Tarney, *What Does the Nursery School Teach?* (Washington D.C.: NAEYC, 106, 1965), p. 71.

[3]K. Read, *The Nursery School: A Human Relationships Laboratory,* 4th ed. (Philadelphia: Saunders, 1966), p. 357.

[4]Logan, *Teaching the Young Child,* p. 107.

firsthand experiences, exposure to equipment and materials, and personal interest and explanations of new ideas, the parent helps the child develop concepts, organize ideas, and broaden horizons.

There are many points that should be considered in planning a home preschool curriculum. Leeper lists the following 14 points that should appear almost daily in some form or another in the child's curriculum:[5]

- Plan together—for the day, for a short period of time, for special events.
- Make decisions—as to work, play, rest, and habits of behavior.
- Learn new skills—as an individual child and in groups with other family members or with friends.
- Expand interests—in special areas or in new areas.
- Have balance—between active and quiet activities and between indoor and outdoor play.
- Have opportunities—to laugh together, to console others, and to help others.
- Have opportunities to work alone—to browse among materials or to think and muse quietly.
- Visit places—within the neighborhood or community, or ask a person from outside the immediate environment to visit.
- Establish routines—of physical habits, work habits, discipline, or self-direction, and self-control.
- Develop social values—following through with an activity and receiving acceptance, developing a balance between independence or initiation and between consideration or aggression, developing a pride in ownership with a willingness to share, and acquiring a feeling of security for self but also a sense of responsibility to others.
- Develop readiness—in reading, speech, communication skills, mathematics, writing, according to the child's maturity.
- Grow—through creative expression in music, rhythm, dramatic play, art activities, games.

[5]S. H. Leeper, R. J. Dales, D. S. Skipper, and R. L. Witherspoon, *Good Schools for Young Children: A Guide for Working with Three, Four, and Five Year Old Children* (New York: Macmillan, 1968), pp. 135-36.

- Explore the natural environment — through observing, investigating, experimenting, and experiencing.
- Provide time for parent — observation and participation.

Good curriculum planning demands that the parent see the relationship between objectives, children, ideas, processes, materials, resources, and organization. The result is desirable learning experiences that have significance in breadth and depth, and learning becomes enjoyable and satisfying for the child.

5
communication skills

*Our children . . . must be well equipped
with words that say what the heart feels.*

Mauree Applegate

the communication skills—listening, speaking, reading, and writing—are more than just the means to social experiences; they are the process by which civilization survives and prospers. They provide the power to think, to create, to express, to interpret, and to evaluate ideas. The child's ability to develop from infancy to adulthood will be greatly enhanced if he learns to be skillful in communication.

> As the child develops in his understanding of the words, as he brings meaning to the symbols through experiences that make words come alive, and as he learns that words are symbols for things and ideas and processes, he will develop a sensitivity to patterns. He will enjoy exploring patterns unlike those he already knows, and he will learn to relate the spoken word to the written symbol.[1]

The parent can guide the child as he learns to associate these new patterns with his daily activities and clothe them in meaning. But such guidance requires that the parent be convinced that the key to understanding one's fellowmen lies in the communication skills.

Communication skills for the young child involve helping the child to express his thoughts, feelings, and ideas. However, before such expressions can be made, a child must have something to express. He must have some prior experiences stored within him to recall, or he must now be experiencing something which he feels a need to express.

Guiding a child in the development of communication skills means more than providing learning experiences which teach the tools of communication, and it is even more than providing a rich experiential background for the child to talk about. It also requires that the parents be responsive to the child's efforts to communicate. It is all too easy for a parent to become preoccupied with the cares of the day and thus miss opportunities to listen to the child's enthusiastic telling of some happening. Communication is not just telling; it is listening and understanding.

[1]Logan, *Teaching the Young Child: Methods of Preschool and Primary Education* (Boston: Houghton Mifflin Co., 1960), p. 171.

listening

And they were learned for they had listening ears.
Author unknown

In our society, listening constitutes the basic tool of learning as well as the major means of social intercourse. We listen three times as much as we read. Listening is the chief means of verbalized learning during the first years of life. Instruction in reading and many other areas is given through oral language. Thus the child's ability to comprehend oral language is vital. Tests show that listening ability has a great effect on developing socially acceptable behavior.

Physical conditions affecting the listener (deafness, hunger, fatigue, illness, and physical environment) can impair the listening process or influence the quality of listening. However, listening is not largely a matter of intelligence. We listen with our experience, not with our intelligence. According to Logan, the relationship between listening and intelligence does not prove to be close. The child who has had rich and varied experiences will be interested in many facets of living; he will have words in his vocabulary to help him comprehend more of what he hears; and thus he will be better equipped to listen.[2]

The environmental climate or atmosphere of the home should motivate listening. The atmosphere should be permissive in that children are free to express their ideas; they should feel that their contributions will be accepted and respected. The parent can take advantage of opportunities for teaching listening and plan specific activities to promote listening skills.

We listen for different reasons, but generally listening may be said to be of three types: (1) appreciative listening to any kind of stimuli pleasing to the sense of the listener; (2) discriminative listening to informative speech for the purpose of comprehension; and (3) critical listening to persuasive speech for the purpose of evaluating the speaker's argument and evidence.

The progressive stages in developing listening skills and behavior are outlined below:[3]

- *Little conscious listening:* The child listens only when he is the center of interest and is easily distracted by people and things.
- *Half-listening:* The child is more interested in his own ideas and waits to break in.
- *Passive listening:* The child just sits, with little or no reaction.
- *Sporadic listening:* The child shows interest if the conversation is closely related to his own experience but shuts off the current when the conversation turns away from him.
- *Listening:* The child reacts through comments or questions.
- *Responsive listening:* The child exhibits indications of sincere emotional and intellectual response.
- *Highest level of listening:* The child completely understands what is being said.

Children listen at one or more of these levels throughout the day. Each year the child should be nearer the highest level of

[2]Logan, *Teaching the Young Child,* p. 173.
[3]Logan, *Teaching the Young Child,* p. 176.

listening as a communication skill. Young children vary in their ability to listen, but every young child can learn basic listening skills as a part of the speech situation. The following pages contain activities to help develop good listening skills.

listening activities

CONVERSATION AND TELEPHONING

Conversation requires listening skills that the child will need during his entire life.

- A child should be encouraged to listen to others not only for information but as an act of courtesy. A child might share interesting happenings with his family or with another person. Remember to set a good example: Listen attentively when the child is speaking.
- Telephoning is particularly appropriate for the young child if it is introduced and supervised properly. Let the child just listen to the dial tone, the busy signal, and the ring. The child will learn to discriminate one sound from another.
- A play telephone might be used at first to let the child dramatize the appropriate responses. A child can set up standards for telephone behavior such as these: Answer correctly; listen attentively; call politely if someone is called to the phone; talk for a brief time; and say good-bye before you hang up. Remember, a child's standards will be a copy of your telephone manners.

DISCUSSION AND PLANNING

Discussing, planning, and evaluating periods call for purposeful listening. Children can make plans for their day: work they need to do, play activities, an outing, a party, or holiday fun. They listen to suggestions from parents and then share their ideas.

DIRECTIONS

Many games and activities require listening skills to understand the procedure.

- A child might be given a series of actions to perform. Give only a few at first, such as, "Clap your hands, and sit down on the green chair." After a child experiences success with a few instructions, give him a longer list, such as "Walk to the center of the room, turn around twice, hop once, return to the red chair, and sit down."
- Give the child directions for drawing on a piece of paper or a chalkboard, such as "Draw a triangle inside another triangle." After success is achieved with this, try giving a series of directions, such as "Make three dots any place on the paper; join the dots with straight lines, and draw a circle inside the joined dots."
- Simon-Says is a good game that requires concentration in listening.
- A series of nonsense syllables, such as be-cil-tee, might be spoken and then repeated by the child in the form of a game, to check listening. The child will enjoy making up his own nonsense syllables and having mother repeat them for him.

DRAMATIC ACTIVITIES AND STORYTELLING

Puppet shows, plays, creative dramatics, flannel-board demonstrations, television and radio programs, and poetry reading are excellent avenues for appreciative listening.

- Read a short paragraph about an animal, and then ask the child to pretend to be the animal and act out what was read in the exact order that it was read. Example: "A lion paced slowly back and forth in its cage. Suddenly he stopped stock still and listened. Then he sniffed the air. Then he gave a low growl and lay down on the floor of his cage." Begin with one or two sentences and increase the number as listening efficiency increases.

- *Dramatize the Action Suggested by a Poem.* After reading the poem aloud, ask the child to act out the various conversations that might have taken place, or let him add his own ideas to the poem.
- *Finish-a-story.* A story is started by someone, and then the child is asked to supply a good ending to the story. This requires attentive listening during the start of the story so that an appropriate ending can be supplied.

MUSICAL ACTIVITIES

Musical activities, such as listening to various instruments, water glasses, chimes, or bells, as well as to recordings and radio programs, improves the child's listening skills and his appreciation for music. (Also see "Music.")

- Auditory Discrimination. Use two sound-makers or instruments such as a drum and a bell. Name each one and demonstrate the sounds made by each. Ask the child to cover his eyes, listen to one sound, and then tell which instrument was used to make the sound. Encourage the child to name the instrument rather than just point. Variations:

  - *Variation #1:* Use two bells, one with a high sound and one with a low sound, such as a cowbell and a Christmas bell.
  - *Variation #2:* Use three or more noisemakers on a table; describe, name, and sound each. Ask the child to cover his eyes, listen to one sound, and then name the instrument used.
  - *Variation #3:* Ask the child to close his eyes while you tap on an object in the room, such as a wooden, metal, glass, or plastic object. Then ask the child to name the object. The child then taps on an object and lets the mother guess.

- "Do This." The mother initiates the game by tapping on the table or a toy drum and asking the child to imitate her. For example, a parent says, "Do this," and then produces one long and two short taps. The child imitates these taps. After some practice the child can be the leader.

- Variation: Various patterns of sound are made by clapping, clicking, etc.
- The parent hums, sings, or plays records of songs that are familiar to the child and asks the child to identify the title of each song.

LISTENING FOR CENTRAL IDEAS OR LISTENING TO THINK

A child can begin early to listen for the central idea in stories or in television or radio programs. A child then takes a main idea from a story and makes up a new story based on that idea.

- Secrets. Whisper something in the child's ear, such as "We will have ice cream for lunch today." The child then repeats the secret in your ear or tells you a secret of his own. Accept any kind of expression as a secret, and enjoy it together with an exchange of knowing looks and laughter. Variations:

  Variation #1: Play the game with other members of the family by repeating a secret to others and then letting the last one tell it aloud to all.

  Variation #2: Place an object in a bag without the child's seeing the object. Whisper the secret of what is in the bag to the child. Then let the child open the bag, checking to see if what he heard is the same as what is in the bag.

- Read a story about a child with one outstanding characteristic, such as laziness or bravery; then ask your child to answer questions, such as "If David lived next door why would (or wouldn't) he make a good friend?"
- Read about an experience, a trip, for example, and then ask the child to explain why he would (or wouldn't) like to go through this experience.
- Describe an animal by telling a riddle. When you have finished instruct the child to draw the animal you have described. Example: "This animal lives along the river and uses the river for his swimming pool. He is short but very fat and heavy, and keeps cool by spending much of his time in the river. His face looks something like a pig's face, and so does his tail. He has

small, popping eyes, small ears, and a hugh mouth with great teeth. You feel like laughing when you see this animal. He looks as if he needs a girdle. What animal am I describing?" (A hippopotamus). To check listening skills, look for detail in the drawings.

- "I Am Thinking of a Word." There are many variations of this game:

    - *Variation #1:* "I am thinking of a word or a phrase that describes exactly how you feel when you are angry." (The child might suggest words like hot, like fighting, like crying, like hitting, and so on.)
    - *Variation #2:* "I am thinking of a long, important word for the way I feel when someone sees me doing something wrong." ("Embarrassed" or "ashamed" might be answers.)
    - *Variation #3:* "I am thinking of a word or words that describe how the boy in this picture might feel." (Use pictures from magazines.)
    - *Variation #4:* "I am thinking of an object in the room." (You describe the object.) "Can you guess what it is?"

SOUNDS ALL AROUND US

Children enjoy listening to sounds about them. Here are some games that call attention to sounds.

- "What Did I Do?" The child is blindfolded. Then the parent or another child performs some action, such as skipping, running, hopping, sliding, jumping, or clapping. The child then tries to relate the noise he heard to the movement. If the child answers correctly, he take a turn at performing the action.
- "Tick, Tock, Where Is the Clock?" Hide a loudly ticking clock while the child covers his eyes. Then ask the child, "Tick, tock, where is the clock?" If played in a group, two or three children may hunt for the clock; the child who finds the clock hides it next.
- Listen and Tell. The child closes his eyes and listens; then he tells what he hears.

- Big Bang, Little Bank. Use objects which make grossly different sounds when dropped, such as keys on a chain, wooden block, spoon, or a cloth doll. Place several of these objects on a table, and drop them one by one with the child watching. Shut your eyes. Ask the child to drop one object while you guess what has been dropped. The child then shuts his eyes and guesses while you drop an object. Variation: Drop one of the objects from high or low. The child then tries to distinguish the height by the loudness of the sound.

- Look and Listen. Line up four toys or articles, such as a block, doll, car, and drum, on a table so the child can see them. Pointing to the articles from left to right, name them as the child looks and listens. Name the articles again but make an apparent mistake, praise the child for being such a good listener. If the child does not detect the mistake, ask him to listen carefully while you repeat the names of the articles with the same apparent mistake. Pictures may be used instead of actual articles. This is a good activity to carry on with a picture book while traveling.

- Tape Recorder Sounds. During a regular day, occasionally turn on a tape recorder and record familiar sounds, such as the telephone ringing, water running, opening and closing of a door, coughing or sneezing, the radio, or the like. Then play back the sounds for the child to identify. Variation: Record familiar voices of family members or friends, and ask the child to identify the person who is talking.

- Tape Recorder — Child's Voice. Establish with the child some guidelines for recording, such as placement of microphone, voice volume, speed of speaking, etc., and then interview the child on the tape. Ask questions, such as "How old are you?" "What color pants do you have on today?" "What color hair do you have?" "What is your favorite food?" Play back the interview as the child listens. Variation: Let the child recite a poem or tell a story on the tape.

- Mother Cat and Kittens (group only). The child who is mother cat chooses three kittens. Mother cat covers her eyes, and then the kittens hide in the room. Mother cat locates the kittens by listening to their meows. When mother cat locates a kitten, she determines the name of the child by the sound of that child's meow.

- What Is This? Imitate a noise, such as an animal's growl or a machine noise, and ask, "What is this?" The child then guesses.

The child will, also enjoy making the sounds and asking you to guess.

- Listening Walk. Go outside for a walk, and listen for all the sounds that can be heard. Before you go, tell the child to listen carefully so he can describe the sounds when you return. Take just a quiet-listening walk — listening for very quiet sounds — or take a loud-listening walk. Be sure to notice where the sounds come from, what kind of sounds they are, how loud they are, and how they make you feel. The child should be able to describe the sound he hears on the listening walk. If you cannot go outside, make it a pretend walk and listen for pretend sounds.

- Drawing Sounds. This activity is especially beneficial after a listening walk. Talk about things that make sounds and the different kinds of sounds — big ones, little ones, long ones, short ones, pleasant ones, harsh ones, gay ones, all kinds of sound. How can you draw these sounds? Crayons will help you. Some sounds are quiet and some colors are quiet. Some sounds are noise and some colors are noisy. Talk about light, quiet colors or bright, loud ones or heavy, dark ones. The child may want to use those colors to make lines that describe the sounds, or he may just want to fill all the space with a picture of a real object that makes the sounds.

LIKENESSES AND DIFFERENCES OF SOUND

To be successful in reading, children should be able to recognize the difference between sounds of words and the difference between sounds of letters in words.

- Sound Cans. Place four different substances — a small block, piece of clay, piece of cotton, small amount of sand — in four identical cans. When all the lids are on, shuffle the cans. The child guesses well.) Allow the child to examine and feel all the substances and When all the lids are on, shuffle the cans. The child guesses what is in each can by hearing noises as they are shaken.

- Parrot Talk. Use a paper-bag puppet of a parrot, or just use your hands and fingers to look like a mouth of a parrot talking.

Discuss with the child how parrots like to repeat everything they hear. Let the child speak first while you are the parrot and repeat everything the child says. Then you speak first and the child repeats. Begin with a single word and build up to a full sentence.

- Nonsensical words may also be used. Variation: Talk to the child about echoes and how they repeat the sounds two or three times. After you have echoed something the child has said or a noise the child has made by tapping, for instance, let the child be your echo.

- Animal Sounds. Tell a story about a farmer who lost his cow and lamb. (You may wish to hold up pictures of the animals you discuss.) "It was night, and the farmer could not see in the dark. He had to use his ears to find his lost cow and lamb. He heard a sound and didn't know if it was a cow or a lamb. What do you think it was?" Make the sound of one of the animals, and let the child give the name of the animal and pick the appropriate picture. Repeat the story with different animals, or change the story to include a zookeeper and zoo animals.

- Add-a-Word. Name two or three words that begin alike, such as fish, farmer, and friend. The child must add a word beginning with the same sound, for example, father or feather.

- Clap if It's Wrong. Start by saying, "Say the word whale softly. How do your lips feel as you begin that work? Now I'm going to say a list of words, some of which are like the word whale. Whenever you hear a word that doesn't begin like whale, clap your hands. Listen carefully: whale, which, where, berry, whistle, man, boat, . . ."

- Think of a Word. Think of a word that rhymes with another word until you have a set of rhyming words: jiggle, giggle, wiggle, or tacks, ax, packs. Ask the child to help you make up sets of rhyming words. Then ask the child if he can put a set of rhyming words into a poem, such as "Children giggle, puddings jiggle, puppies wiggle."

- Ryming Colors. Choose a color that describes something and rhymes with it: pink sink, blue shoe, red sled, green bean, black sack, yellow fellow, and the like. Ask the child to think up his own combinations.

- Sound-alike Words. Ask the child to put sounds together: "I'm thinking of a word that begins like where and ends like hen."

(When) Or, "I'm thinking of a word that begins like blink and ends like pack." (Black)

- Compound Words. Say, "I'm thinking of a word. The first part rhymes with go and is cold and white; the second part rhymes with ball, and we often do it when we're shating. What is the word?" (Snowfall) Make up other compound words before the child tries to make up some of his own.

- Rhyming Words. The child listens to a nursery rhyme or poem and repeats the rhyming words. Example: Jill and hill, cat and rat, etc.

- Same or Different. Say words like three and free, and ask the child if they are the same words or different words. Do the same with ship and chip, chair and share, witch and which. Occasionally use the same word twice in a one word pair.

- "Which Word Is Different?" Say four words, three with the same beginning sound and one that is different. Ask which word starts with a different sound. Examples: mice, fish, money, mouse; fire, fat, dog, fence, top, tent, cat, tool.

- "Let's Make Up a Rhyme." Encourage the child to make up simple rhymes, such as "The little white cat wore a pink hat."

oral expression

*First find something to say
and then find something to say it with.*
Arnold Newman

The child's language instruction begins the moment he hears a spoken word. Language is such an important aspect of every person's life that it is natural for emphasis on its mastery to begin almost as soon as a child is born. Many educators feel that the skills of oral communication are prerequisite to the development of all language skills.

Because the child tends to imitate those about him, he naturally learns to speak the language he hears. His vocabulary, usage, articulation, and pronunciation are inevitably patterned after those of his parents or others in his immediate environment. However, no child immediately learns to say words exactly as he hears them said, whether they be baby talk or flawless English. A child's vocal mechanism must mature and become adjusted to making the required and meaningful sounds. This adjustment is a gradual process and varies with different children. But as a child grows, he learns to say words as he has heard them said. Thus the young child readily develops habits of good or bad oral expression as he imitates his environment.

The family environment plays the most important part in determining the quality of the language facility he develops and the speed with which he develops it. The child whose parents talk to him a great deal develops facility earlier than the child who plays alone or has only limited contact with adults. The child needs opportunities to gain new ideas and concepts. Going to the park, visiting the zoo, taking vacation trips, traveling extensively with parents, or even accompanying his mother on shopping expeditions can help the child acquire a wealth of new sights and sounds, as well as the words that relate to them. A child whose parents read good books to him gains experiences available in no other way.

The home environment should give the child much to talk about, but in addition, parents must foster spontaneity in expression and provide opportunities to be heard and appreciated. A parent can help by entering into the child's conversations, offering friendly comments, and giving a great deal of encouragement.

The best way to foster expression, to develop adequate vocabularies, and to help the child learn new concepts is to provide opportunities for interesting experiences with new words. The attitudes and skills of parents are the significant factors in the development of sensitivity to words. Many parents are steeped in the tradition of reading good literature. They like to read, and they enjoy beautiful language. Others are not so fortunate; however, parents can learn along with their children to appreciate the beauty of language and to feel the excitement of discovering a new word that is just right for the situation. Parents who take pains to always talk on a child's level create a sterile, unimaginative vocabulary. Children love new words, especially the big ones. They should occasionally have to rise to the necessity of gathering word meaning from context. Parents will be surprised at the adroitness of children in doing this.

oral-expression
activities

USAGE, ARTICULATION,
AND PRONUNCIATION

Young children enjoy playing with words and sounds. Parents can exploit this natural tendency to improve the child's ability to distinguish among sounds and to enunciate sound combinations accurately.

- Make a familiar animal sound—of a cat, dog, duck, kitten, rooster, pig. Ask the child to name the animal, and then allow the child to make the sound of another animal while the adult guesses.
- Tell the child to say a new word as slowly as possible, then as quickly as possible.
- Have the child imitate sounds of animals, airplanes, trains, clocks, and the like.
- Tell or read a story, with the child putting appropriate objects on a flannel board when they are mentioned in the story and naming each object as they do so.
- Tell or read a story involving animals, and instruct the child to make the sound of the particular animal whenever that animal is mentioned.
- Play games requiring different types of voices: A young child's tiny voice, a father's big deep voice, or a grandfather's shaky voice.
- Provide opportunities for dramatic play and simple puppet shows. (See "Dramatic Play.")
- Use finger plays to help the child hear and pronounce the sounds correctly. (See Appendix B: Finger Plays).
- Help the child with the particular sounds he cannot say. Show him how to position his lips and tongue to make the sound. Ask him to listen to the sound in jingles and rhymes and then practice it in easy, monosyllabic words. Praise his progress!

53

- Use tongue twisters for practice in articulation. Examples:

  — Crackers crackle, crackers crumble.
  — Try tying twine to three tree twigs.
  — Sixty sticky thumbs.
  — Slippery soap suds.

INFORMAL SHARING OF IDEAS

A child needs opportunities and encouragement in order to develop effective oral communication.

- Use speech to talk it out when a child feels hostile. Let the child express his inner feelings. Be sure to listen to what he is trying to say as well as to what he actually says.
- Help the child to talk about things of interest to him:

  — Losing a tooth.
  — A new baby brother or sister.
  — Games or favorite toys.
  — Favorite stories or books.
  — A picture he has drawn.
  — A pet he has or one he would like to have, and what he does or would do to care for that pet.
  — Activities, special events, such as parties or outings planned with the child's help, and what he enjoyed most about each.

- Children like to imitate adults through dramatic play. Both boys and girls play house and take the role of dentist, car salesmen, grocer, restaurant owner, or doctor. As they assume these roles, they have an opportunity to express themselves in the guise of an adult.
- Dramatizations of stories, nursery rhymes, and poems gives the child opportunities to appear in various roles.
- Use a play or real telephone to give the child an opportunity to speak and carry on real or imaginary conversations.
- Let the child pretend he is speaking on television by standing

behind a large picture frame or a large box with the front and back cut out and control knobs drawn on to resemble a television set.

- Let the child tell stories by using ready-made felt designs and figures, or let him make his own felt designs to retell a story.
- Arrange for the child to dictate a letter or story to an adult while the adult writes it on a large chart to be posted in an important place.
- Using large newsprint and felt pens, write down the child's news of the day as he relates it to you. The child may then draw a picture of his news below the written words. Post the newspaper in an important place. Let the child read his newspaper to other members in the family.
- Allow the child to serve as host or hostess when company comes. Help the child to make simple introductions, such as introducing a friend to you, and teach the child how to greet strangers. Help the child to express his appreciation for an enjoyable visit or party.
- Ask the child to make up a game and explain the directions.
- Make a recording of the child talking or singing and give it to someone special as a gift.

VOCABULARY DEVELOPMENT

An adequate vocabulary is of tremendous importance to understanding what one reads and also in expressing one's ideas. Studies show a significantly high correlation between the size of a person's vocabularly and his ability to read—even his success in life and economic status.

Develop sensory words, words related to seeing, hearing, feeling, smelling, and tasting. (See also "Our Bodies.")

Seeing

- Go for a "color walk." Look for things of one color, such as all the red things or all the blue things. After the child has mastered the major colors, you can talk about the light blue of the sky and the dark blue of a particular car.

- Use housework as learning times together. Talk about size and shape while making the bed. Let the child help you sort the laundry into light-and-dark-colored items.

- Mix food coloring to make different colors. Let the child experiment, with supervision. Help the child verbalize what is happening.

- Have the child sort buttons into egg cartons according to color, number of holes, or size.

- Call attention to the shapes in the house, such as rectangles: windows, doors, table top, and TV screen; or circles: wheels on toys, clock, coins, and shape of mouth when saying "oh."

- Ask the child to close his eyes while you place one common article, such as a hair brush, comb, toothbrush, bar of soap, book, pencil, or piece of paper, under an inverted box. The child open his eyes and you remove the box and say, "One, two, three!" Then replace the box over the article, and ask, "What did you see?" The child tries to tell as quickly as possible. After presenting several articles in the same category, you might ask, "How are these articles alike?" A variation: Use the same item in different colors, such as socks, and ask the child to tell the color. Or use geometric shapes and ask the child to tell the shape.

- Play the game I-spy by describing an item in the room and then allowing the child to guess what has been described. The child can then describe an item in the room or elsewhere while you guess.

Hearing (See also "Listening Activities.")

- Ask the child to close his eyes. Make a sound, such as the crumpling of paper, humming a tune, slamming a door, or opening and closing books. The child tries to identify the sound and then thinks of words to describe the sound. Then reverse the roles.

- Talk with the child about the sounds around the house and yard. Listen to the sounds of rain, wind blowing, children playing, water running, and airplanes overhead. Talk about the different sounds heard in different places—loud and soft sounds, fast- and slow-paced sounds. Ask the child to reproduce the sounds that he hears.

Feeling

- Let the child help achieve the right temperature of water for his bath. Talk about more hot water and more cold water.
- When eating, talk about how food feels in the mouth—soft, scratchy, dry, hard, rough, or chewy.
- Collect several items, such as a piece of fur, a square of sandpaper, a rock, and some damp spaghetti. Ask how each item feels, and then allow the child time with each item to explore descriptive words.
- Blindfold the child and present him with an item of clothing, such as a sweater, coat, pair of pants, or shoelace. Ask the child to describe the article. Ask him to find various parts of each item, such as the buckle and holes on a belt, belt loops and zipper on a pair of pants, top button on a sweater, and the like. Talk about names for articles of clothing and their parts.
- Let the child reach into a cloth bag (pillowcase) in which some item, such as a toy airplane, ball, piece of sandpaper, rock, cotton ball, paper clip, or toothbrush, has been placed. Using descriptive words, ask the child questions about what he feels: "Is the object cuddly?" "Is it fuzzy?" "Is it heavy?" Then let the child describe how the object feels to him. The child then guesses what the object is.

Smelling

- Take a "smelling walk." Notice freshness of the air, fresh paint, the odor of animals, the fragrance of plants and flowers, and the scent of the soil. Think of words that describe each smell. A variation: If you cannot go outside, take a "smelling walk" in your kitchen. Smell soap, vinegar, vanilla, bread, and other grocery items.
- When dinner is cooking, ask the child if he can tell what is cooking. Ask the child to describe the smell: "Does it smell sweet? Is the smell strong or faint?" Fill the child's plate, cover his eyes, and ask him to guess what food is on the plate. Tell him to compare the smells of various foods.

Tasting

- Present a "secret food" in a paper bag so that the child cannot see it. Give the child some descriptive taste words to help him guess what is in the bag: sour, juicy, cold, delicious, and the like. After the child has guessed, ask the child to select a food to put in the bag and then describe the food to you in the form of a riddle.

• Ask the child to close his eyes, and then allow him to sample foods of the same kind but with different tastes, such as sweet foods: marshmallows, cinnamon candies, and chocolate cookies. After the child has tasted one, ask, "How does it taste?" After he has tasted the second, ask, "Does this taste the same? How is it different?" Try this with sour, crunchy, soft, mild, sharp, wet, or dry foods.

• Serve a meal including foods of one color but of varied tastes, such as cherry gelatin, strawberry dessert, raspberry drink, spaghetti with tomato sauce, beets, and tomatoes. Discuss the variety of tastes and the similarities in color.

ACTIVITIES FOR VOCABULARY DEVELOPMENT

• "Let's Learn the Name." In museums, zoos, or parks, tell the child the names of the objects while he is seeing them. Use specific names for objects such as trees: maple, sycamore, oak, or pecan.

• Read stories to the child to help him increase his vocabulary. Help the child learn more specific words for verbs:

    — Walked — trotted, hobbled, strutted, minced, marched.
    — Talked — whispered, exclaimed, shouted, muttered.
    — Looked — peered, gazed, stared.

• Make picture dictionaries or notebooks with the child by collecting pictures of objects.

• Make collections of rocks, leaves, and insects with the child. Help him learn the names of many of the objects and the names of some of the parts of the objects.

• Encourage hobbies to add words to the child's vocabulary.

• Look at pictures in books and magazines. Encourage the child to ask the names of objects that he does not know.

• When the child plays with building blocks, help him call objects by name: cylinders, cubes, rectangles, squares, triangles, and circles.

- Give the child an opportunity to use newly learned words freely in conversation.

- Let the child act out the meaning of new words such as scampered, gazed, stamped, or hobbled.

- Make a play store, and discuss the parts of the store and the objects in it: the fresh-vegetable department, which contains asparagus, cauliflower, green beans, and other items; the cereal department, which contains oatmeal and bran flakes; and so forth.

- Learn names of objects in a room, such as venetian blinds, drapes, or furnace. Put labels on the items talked about.

- Listen to records with the child, to help increase his vocabulary.

- Ask him to sing new songs, to help him learn new words.

- Collect and classify words with him:

  - Elephant words—clumsy, weighty, huge, massive, immense, heavy.
  - Funny words—laugh, giggle, joy, delight, silly, hilarious, jovial.
  - Heavy words—fat, full, solid, strong, cumbersome, obese, ton.
  - Soft words—cuddly, fuzzy, furry, light, weak, tender, soothing.

- Tell or read a story, leaving out words occasionally and letting the child fill in with his own words.

- A list of "leads" based on words that are emotionally charged helps a child express his feelings. Examples:

  - My friend is _____.
  - I love my grandmother because she is _____.
  - Winning a game makes me feel _____.
  - Losing a game makes one feel _____.
  - My father is _____.

- Ask weather questions: "Do you feel any different when the sun is shining than when the world is cloudy and dusky? Let's think of some words that tell how each kind of weather makes us feel."

Seek to elicit big, powerful words, like energetic, gloomy, and the like.

- Ask the child to respond to incomplete statements about scenery, such as "The mountain looks like _____," or, "The most beautiful sight in the world is _____." Ask the child to describe each in detail.

- Anecdotes about weather situations encourage vocabulary expansion: "Did you ever have a picnic in the rain, or a fishing trip in a storm? Can you tell how you felt? Was it hilarious, exciting, or frightening?"

- Tell the child to choose a favorite character from a story that has been read to him. Ask him to make up a riddle about that character to test your ability to guess the character. Then you can describe a character familiar to the child and ask the child to guess. Play tape recordings of voices, and then talk about the voices. Ask the child if the voices are high, low, gruff, rasping, loud, soft, angry, or pleasing.

- The movements of people provide an interesting source of contrasts. Ask the child to pantomime a sloucher, a shuffler, a runner, or an ambler. Then use the sitting position in a similar way for him to imitate people as they sprawl, lounge, or slump.

- Do not forget the mood and personality-trait words. Ask, "How do you describe a person—cheerful, talkative, vivacious, energetic. Make up some imaginary people for the child to describe.

- Use pictures from magazines to develop words pertaining to size. People aren't just short or tall, fat or slim, big or little: They are obese, immense, huge, and gigantic.

- Ask the child for some words that describe the sounds, sights, smells, and movements of the big city, the country, a circus, or the ocean.

- Prepare silhouettes together. Instruct the child to lie down on a piece of heavy brown wrapping paper on the floor, legs and arms open. Draw around his body with chalk or pencil. The child then paints the figure according to what he is wearing or what he would like to be wearing. As the child colors, discuss the parts of the body, joints, colors, various articles of clothing, and the like.

reading readiness

*. . . And I opened it and turned pages and held
it near a window and had my wondering about how
those black marks on white paper could be words
your eyes would pick off into words your tongue
would speak.*
Carl Sandburg

Words are the symbols of man's ideas and his reactions to
the world in which he lives. Words merely serve to convey the ideas
and to clothe them. Words come to life as they are associated
with experience and with meaning. Effective communication of
ideas in reading comes only when the reader brings meaning and
experience to the printed page.

Up to this point in the child's life, he has read symbols other
than printed words. He has read expressions on the faces of people
around him, he has read the symbols of nature, and he has read
oral symbols. All this previous reading of symbols will aid him in
his introduction to written symbols.[4]

[4]Logan, *Teaching the Young Child,* p. 183.

It is important to be aware of the child's desire to know what the written symbols mean, for this is an essential element in the process of reading to learn. Generally, if a child has an interest in and enthusiasm for reading for a purpose, the process is free of many of the difficulties inherent in teaching a child who is not eager.

Reading readiness refers to the factors that determine the probable success of an individual in reading. These factors are classified under four headings: physical, social, emotional, and mental. (See "Appendix A: Checklist for Reading Readiness" to help determine which readiness activities are most needed for your child.)

reading readiness activities

PHYSICAL READINESS

The physical readiness of the child is dependent upon his physical development, his general health, and lack of defects. Such aspects of development as hearing, vision, speech, physical control, muscular coordination, effects of childhood disease, and present state of health should be carefully examined. The following are suggestions for improving the child's daily health habits and physical development:

- Ask the child to cut out pictures of people brushing their teeth from magazines and make a picture collage to post in a conspicuous place.
- Help the child develop a regular health routine, such as washing hands before eating and brushing teeth after eating, so he learns it is always done.
- Put the child's name on his own things: washcloth, towel, toothbrush, and other personal items.
- Make a health chart, listing things the child can do for himself, such as washing hands, flushing the toilet, and covering his

mouth when coughing. Give a star or make a check on a chart each time the child performs a good health habit.

- Give the child fruit or raw vegetables instead of candy as a snack. Do things with the child, for example, climbing stairs and jumping down them one at a time. Go for walks and step on the cracks — or avoid the cracks. Jump over or onto the cracks in the sidewalks. Race to the corner and back (running, fast walking, hopping, skipping), do somersaults, roll down hills, and the like.
- Ask the child to walk forward and backward on a curb or along a crack in the sidewalk.
- Play catch with your child, using a ball at least six inches in diameter to start with. Throw large balls into an empty basket or garbage can.
- For activities that develop small-muscle control, see "writing readiness."

SOCIAL READINESS

Social interaction is important at this time in a child's life; a whole new world of cooperation, sharing, and self-reliance is beginning to unfold for him. A child who does not feel comfortable in these areas of relationships cannot be free to expand his skills. The following are suggestions for improving the child's social readiness as he becomes more independent in his everyday life and develops positive social attitudes:

- Set aside definite places for things in the home. Let the child help straighten up and put things away. Place clothes hooks or hangers low enough so the child can hang up his own clothes. Provide a shelf or toy box so that the child has a place to put toys.
- Allow the child to dress himself. Let him choose, within limits, what to wear.
- Give the child a special job and then praise the effort made, even if it is not done to perfection. A child might set the table, dust the furniture, put away the broom, and clear his dishes from the table.
- Give the child real choices, usually between two items: which of two books he would like you to read from, which of two foods would he like for a snack, and so on.

- Help the child to complete one thing before going on to something else.
- Provide opportunities for the child to share something he has done or made with others. Be sure to let the child know that you are willing to share your time and things with him.
- Help the child to be considerate of others, their feelings, and their property. For example, you might ask, "How does John feel when you do that?"
- Provide opportunities for the child to give gifts or special remembrances to family members and friends.
- Talk positively to the child about teachers, neighbors, and others.

EMOTIONAL READINESS

Emotional readiness is closely interwoven with aspects of physical, social, and mental development. Evidence of withdrawal, hostility, restlessness, lack of concentration, lack of self-esteem, negative reactions to others, negative reactions to new experiences, and unwillingness to read indicates a lack of emotional readiness for reading. Parental rejection, a broken home, and maladjustment to relationships in the home contribute to feelings of insecurity that may result in an emotional unreadiness for reading. The following are ideas for developing and sustaining emotional readiness:

- Comment on any change in the child's behavior that you like: "I like it when you put away your toys so quickly." "I am glad you tried to ride your bike." "I like the way you combed your hair."
- Take pictures of your child and keep a photo album. This may be just a few sheets of paper stapled together. Show the child the pictures and talk about the pictures with him.
- Talk and listen to the child alone each day, at a special time, if possible.
- Let the child choose some favorite foods to have at dinner. Tell the family, "We are having hot dogs because John wanted them." Let the child help you prepare things he likes, such as cookies, and let him know you are making them because he likes them.

- Talk about what the child did when he was a baby and how much he has grown.
- Talk about how the child is the same as other children and how he is different from other children.
- Talk about your family—special things you all like to do, things that are important to each person, special days, and so on.
- Let the child draw himself and members of his family. Talk about the pictures and the members of the family. Ask, "Who else in the family looks like you? Who has the same color of eyes as you? Who has the same color of hair as you?"
- Let a child have some things of his very own that will be protected by adults, if necessary. For example, the child may have a prized doll, truck, or other toy that he should not be required to share with others.
- Take time to find out as specifically as possible how the child is feeling. Help the child find words to describe his emotions.
- Talk about things that make the child happy, sad, scared, or angry.
- Watch TV without sound and talk about how people seem to be feeling. Discuss pictures showing emotions, and make up a story about one of them: "Why does he feel this way? What do you want to happen next? How do you feel when he does that?"
- Have the child draw faces expressing emotions, and then talk about the faces and the reason the person in the picture might feel that way. Ask the child if he has ever felt that way and if so, why.
- Listen to music on a record player or radio, and ask the child how he feels when he hears that kind of music.

MENTAL READINESS

The most significant kind of evaluation for mental readiness is an observation of the child to discover the extent of the child's desire to read, his interest in books, his ability to listen to stories, and his fluency in oral expression and comprehension. The various readiness tests purport to test proficiency in skills such as following directions; interpreting illustrations; seeing likenesses and differences in words; discriminating between word forms; recognizing sound elements, forms of objects, numbers, and words; and comprehending common words and common things. Most if not all these skills are learned as a result of a rich experiential background.

Each day is rich with opportunities for learning many things that later give meaning to the printed word; the child brings meaning to it. He interprets everything he sees, smells, hears, feels, and tastes in terms of his own experience, and draws upon it to bring meaning to the printed symbols. The wider experience he has and the more opportunities to work with others, to talk, to make things, to experiment, to manipulate, to create, and to solve problems, the more eager he will be to add yet another method of extending his knowledge of life.

Some specific ways in which parents can help their children be mentally ready for the adventure of reading follows.

Create a Love for Reading

A child learns most readily those things for which he has developed an interest.

- Provide opportunities for the child to see adults reading. Let him see and know of the joy the parents receive from reading.
- Allow the child to visit libraries and to browse through children's books.
- Allow the child to visit bookstores and buy some books of his very own.
- If possible, allow the child to speak with an author of children's books and discuss the books he or she has written.
- Make many attractive books available to the child, and encourage him to look at the pictures.
- Read stories and poems often to the child.
- Talk to the child about stories, poems, or nursery rhymes.
- Encourage the child to look at children's magazines and make some available.
- Let the child see you turn to encyclopedias, dictionaries, and other books to find answers to some of their questions.

Firsthand Experiences

It is a generally accepted fact that people learn best through direct or firsthand experiences, by seeing things in their natural environment. Excursions provide one of the most useful means for increasing the child's knowledge of life and events outside his immediate environment. There are many places of interest to visit.

Many activities help prepare the child for an excursion. Or if excursions are not feasible, the activities may substitute for the excursion. (See also "Social Studies Excursions.")

- Bring objects into the home and place them in a special display area for the child to view and handle.

  - Flowers. Teach the child to call them by their names (daisy, rose, and so on.)
  - Leaves. Note shape, size, color, veins, and texture.
  - Food. Classify foods as to vegetables, fruits, meats, and the like.
  - Rocks. Classify them as to size, shape, and color.
  - Animals. Classify them as to size, environment, and eating habits.
  - Materials. Call different kinds by their names: cotton, wool, rayon, and nylon.
  - Grains. Categorize them as rice, wheat, corn, and the like.

- Look at and interpret pictures. The child can form many concepts from pictures. Collect pictures and make picture dictionaries by finding pictures of one subject, such as animals, shapes, foods, and plants.
- Tell and read stories about various places.
- Arrange for the child to talk to resource people about their jobs or experiences.
- Let the child look at books on a variety of subjects and places.

Excursions

Establish possible objectives for each visit. Be prepared with some questions to ask the child. Help make the child aware of comparisons or relationships during the trip. After returning home the child may want to relive the experience through dramatic play or by drawing pictures and making a scrapbook about the trip. The following are some suggestions for excursions:

FARMS AND RANCHES

- Dairy farms
- Orchards
- Cattle and sheep ranches
- Chicken or turkey farms
- Flower gardens
- Vegetable gardens
- Pastures
- Woods, rivers, creeks, and lakes

LOCAL BUSINESSES

- Department stores
- Greenhouses
- Bakeries
- Supermarkets
- Pet shops
- Drugstores
- Flower shops
- Barber shops
- Restaurants
- Cafeterias
- Hotels and motels
- Laundromats
- Theaters

COMMUNITY-SERVICE FACILITIES

- Airports
- Police stations
- Fire stations

- Post offices
- Railroad stations
- Courthouses
- School and city libraries
- Bus stations
- Banks
- Hospitals

OTHER FACILITIES

- Zoos
- Docks
- Buildings under construction
- Parks
- Circuses
- Elevators and escalators
- Sites for parties and picnics
- Art galleries
- State capitols
- Museums

Developing a Capacity for Critical and Sustained Listening. (See "Listening.")

Developing Auditory Discrimination. (See "Listening.")

Developing Adequate Speaking Vocabulary. (See "Vocabulary Development.")

VISUAL DISCRIMINATION

The ability to recognize likenesses and differences must be acquired before a child can learn to read words.

- Discuss with the child the differences between cars, boats, airplanes, and trucks. Also discuss their uses.

- Discuss with the child the various models of cars. Show how one model, for instance, is like another model and then how the models differ. Point out only gross differences at first, and then let the child discover more subtle differences.

- Observe differences between buildings in the country and those in the city.

- Let the child see differences in colors and learn the names of the colors. Play color games: sorting colored squares, finding specific colors in the room, matching buttons to fabrics by color, and sorting colored buttons into egg cartons.

- Classify pieces of colored paper according to color and shape.

- Put labels on the child's possessions, and point out differences in the shape of words such as, Jimmy, Mother, Dad, and Sue.

- Instruct the child to draw pictures of himself and a friend, his home and a friend's home, and his pet and a neighborhood pet.

- Classify objects for the purpose of seeing how things are alike and how they differ: trees (maple, oak, sycamore); dogs (collie, dachshund, bulldog), and so on.

- Mount a picture from a magazine or coloring book onto construction paper. Cut this picture in four to eight parts for a jigsaw puzzle. Ask the child to reconstruct the picture.

- Show pictures of four objects of which three are alike and one different. Let the child find the one that is different. The pictures can be gummed stickers purchased from a dime store.

- Show pictures of objects that are all alike except for color, shape, or size.

- Show the child pictures of things with missing parts: a rabbit with only one ear or a cat with only one eye.

- When the child is playing with building blocks, ask him to find all the triangular blocks, squares, rectangles, circles, cylinders, cubes, arches, and other shapes. Or have the child sort the blocks into boxes, each labeled with a silhouette of one shape.

- If a child has built something like a gas station with his blocks, it enriches his play if you make a sign reading "Larry's Gas Station" for him to tape to his building. He might display signs staying "Gas" and "Air" for his pumps. If he has built a street in front of the station, he might use a street sign. The more words a child sees and has defined for him—whether or not he recognizes that word a second later—the more he understands that written words stand for spoken words.

- When the child asks you to look at his block building, when he is particularly engrossed in his work, or when you see a particularly exciting construction, you have an opportunity to take down dictation from the child. If you ask him, "Would you like to tell me about your building?" the chances are that he will have a great deal to tell you. As he talks, take down his story word for word. Watching you take down his story reinforces the idea that written words are symbols and that these symbols are different from each other, just as they sound different from each other. Seeing his own spoken words transformed into written ones makes reading all the more tantalizing. Moreover, it helps the child learn to organize his thoughts and speak well as he dictates to you.

- Ask the child to draw a man or a woman. The picture should be evaluated by the number of details added to the picture (arms, fingers, legs, eyes, nose, and mouth). Help the child take notice of such details.

- Fill a box with objects or pictures that begin with the same letter. Let the child take out the objects one by one, saying the names. Then ask, "How are these objects alike?" Compare these objects with the objects in a box full of C's or any other letter. This may be particularly useful in helping the child distinguish between two difficult sounds, such as B and D. Then the child might file mixed-up objects in the proper boxes—dolls in the D box, cars in the C box, and so on. Tell the child to make up a story with many B words, using the B objects in the story. Then ask him to find other objects in the room that would belong in a box of B's.

- Label items around the room so that the child becomes aware that words have meaning. The child also begins to understand that different sounds look different when written.

- Lotto games. Set small picture cards and master cards containing six to ten pictures each before the child. Ask the child to match each small picture card to a master card. (The pictures have different subjects—animals, household objects, and so forth. Lotto games are available commercially.)

- Picture-domino games. Make or buy small cardboard cards with two separate pictures per card, for example, a star at one end of the card and a heart at the other. The game is played like dominoes, except that the child matches pictures rather than dots.

- Combination card games. Provide small cardboard cards with

pictures of objects such as cups, saucers, desks, chairs, coats, and hats. The child places pictures of objects that go together in the same pile: cups with saucers, desks with chairs, and so forth.

- Rhyming-words game. Provide objects or pictures of objects whose names rhyme, for example, star and car, house and mouse, and tail and whale. Instruct the child to place objects or pictures in rhyming groups.
- Encourage the child to make scrapbooks. The kinds are limited only by the imagination: animals, objects that have the same beginning sounds, objects that are the same color, objects that are used together, and so on.
- Draw incomplete circles, squares, or triangles of different sizes, and ask the child to complete the figures.
- Make a floor plan of your house, and label special places. Make a plan of your yard; label house, play area, equipment, and grass area.

PICTURE INTERPRETATION

It is important for the child to be able to see and interpret pictures and to be able to talk rather fluently about what he sees. If a child cannot keep his mind on pictures, he probably is not ready to learn to read, for it is unlikely that he can keep his mind on a story.

- Show the child pictures and ask him to tell what he sees.
- In two or more pictures that tell a story, help the child to look at the pictures from left to right, to understand what happens first and what happens next.
- Lead the child to comment on the action of each character in the pictures.
- Lead the child to comment on the feelings or emotions that the characters in the pictures may experience.
- Prepare about four pictures to illustrate a story. After you have read the story to the child, ask the child to arrange the pictures in the order the story unfolds.
- Ask the child to interpret three pictures and tell a story from the pictures.

MECHANICS OF READING

Children do not inherently know that a line of print or the letters in a word should be read from left to right. They must train their eyes to make the proper movements.

- When you are reading to the child point out that you begin reading to the left of the page and continue reading toward the right.
- Show the child his name in print and later show him other words. Glide you finger under the word from left to right to show him how to "see" the word.
- Let the child see you write some words, to help him start at the left and proceed to the right.
- When the child picks up a pencil or crayon, help him "write" from left to right.
- When pointing out things on charts, start at the left. Glide your finger under a line of print from left to right.
- Use left-to-right movements in reading and interpreting pictures.
- Play games, such as Simon-says, emphasizing movements to the left and to the right.
- Sing songs, such as "Looby Lou" or "I Put My Right Hand In," giving left and right directions. Example: Skip, hop, walk, or jump three times to the left; three times to the right; and so forth.
- Show the child how to make a return sweep after reading one line by returning to the left of another line. Show the child the margins of a book, spaces between the lines, and spaces between words.
- Children love to cook, so make a recipe chart employing pictures of the ingredients. Read each picture step with the child, moving your hand from left to right.

SPECIAL MENTAL TASKS

Comparing, making assumptions, problem solving, applying principles to new situations, summarizing, and hypothesizing are all mental tasks that relate to the understanding of the printed page.

- Ask the child to compare similarities and differences in two animals from a story, such as Father Bear and Baby Bear in the *Goldilocks and the Three Bears* or two of the pigs in the *Three Little Pigs*.
- Ask the child to compare two people in a story, such as Snow White and Sleepy in *Snow White and the Seven Dwarfs,* or Cinderella and her stepmother in *Cinderella.*
- Ask the child to compare mother's work with father's work.
- Show your child two different containers, each with a different shape and each containing a quantity of water. Ask which contains more water. Help the child to understand that the only accurate way to determine which container holds more water is to measure it.
- Show the child the good side of a wormy or bruised apple. Ask if it is a good apple. Ask how he can tell if it is good.
- Show the child a large box and a smaller box. The larger one may be empty and the smaller one may contain two books. Ask which is heavier. Ask the child how he could really decide which box is heavier.
- Present a situation that requires a solution to a problem. But in addition, give the child some data. The child is then required to work out the solution. Example: "How can we find out which objects in this room contain iron and steel?" We know that a magnet picks up objects of iron and steel. Give the child a magnet to make his discoveries.
- Try riddles to increase the child's ability to solve problems. There are many possibilities for What-am-I? games. Besides the ones below, try riddles for milk, bird, cow, hen, cat, dog, rabbit, duck, horse, fish, and pig.

I come from the sky.
I come in drops.
I wash houses.
I wash trees.
I help make things grow.
I feed rivers.
I fall on umbrellas.
What am I? (Rain)

I am in the sky.
I help make things grow.

I grow on a plant.
I am hard.
Sometimes I am hot.
I go pop, pop, pop.
Then I am white.
Boys like me.
Girls like me.
What am I? (Popcorn)

I am yellow.
I am made from milk.

I put color in the flowers.
I am bright.
I am hot.
I shine in the day time.
People like me.
What am I? (Sun)

I am good to eat.
Boys like me in the summer.
Girls like me in the summer.
I am made of cream.
I am made with ice.
I am cold.
What am I? (Ice cream)

I make noise.
You can hear me.
You cannot see me.
I make ships go.
What am I (Wind)

I am round.
I am red.
I am juicy.
I grow on a tree.
I am good to eat.
What am I? (Apple)

Sometimes I am soft.
Sometimes I am hard.
I am good to eat.
I am put on bread.
What am I? (Butter)

I am white.
I have a shell.
My shell may break.
People like me.
I am good to eat.
The hen lays me.
What am I? (Egg)

I come from the sky.
I am white.
I am cold.
I fall softly.
What am I? (Snow)

I can fly.
I make honey.
I say, "Buzz, buzz."
What am I? (Bee)

- Describe a situation and then ask the child to predict the outcome of the given circumstances. The child is then asked to give his reasons for his prediction. "What would happen if you ate only cookies all day? Why do you think so?"
- Ask the child to watch a television program and then summarize the program.
- Ask the child to summarize the events of a trip or a visit.
- Ask the child to summarize a story that has been read to him.
- Let the child think of a title for a story he has heard.
- Ask the child to suggest titles or captions for pictures in magazines.
- Put the child's imagination to work. Hypothesizing from literature might be suggested with the following examples:

— Cinderella was very unhappy. Why do you think her step-
sisters treated her in such a crude way?

— Peter Pan could fly. How do you think this happened?

— Why do you think Jack sold his cow for only a few beans?

— Why do you think that the duck and the dog and the cat
did not want to help the Little Red Hen plant her wheat?

• Ask the child why a plant kept in the home is dying.

• Show a picture of a man dressed in a business suit. Ask the child,
"What do you think his job is?"

• Help the child to make decisions by asking questions, such as "If
you had $100.00 what would you do?" "If you could do anything
you pleased today, what would it be?" "What is the most beautiful thing you have ever seen?"

writing readiness

*One day you will write a poem which everyone
will read, but first you must learn how to handle
the material from which poems are created.*

Nagol

Even though formal writing instruction does not begin until
after the preschool years, there are many opportunities available
during the preschool years for developing an awareness of the
purpose of writing and its values. The purpose of writing is to
communicate or to express ideas. This purpose is so often lost in
the beginning stages of practice; handwriting is a tool, a means to
an end.[5]

Handwriting is a developmental process, and because children
vary in muscular coordination, many are not ready for formal
writing until sometime in the first grade. Yet, even the preschool
child is interested in this tool of communication and enjoys dictating
stories to a parent. These stories can be written for the child to see
and to share. The preschool child is pleased to discover that writing

[5]S. H. Leeper, R. J. Dales, D. S. Skipper and R. L. Witherspoon, *Good Schools
for Young Children: A Guide for Working with Three, Four, and Five Year Old
Children* (New York: Macmillan, 1968), p. 180.

is "talk written down," and he likes to see his own ideas take shape as the adult writes.

Along with experiences that help to establish a need for writing, the child should use clay, finger paints, easel paints and brushes, blocks, crayons, hammers and nails, puzzles, paste, and many other media. Through these experiences, the child is doing exercises that involve arm and finger movement, eye-hand coordination and muscular control, all of which are essential to learning to write. The specific activities that aid in writing-readiness are as follows:

writing-readiness activities

WRITING HAS MEANING

Children learn the purpose and value of writing as they see it used to help them express their ideas and fulfill their needs.

- Print the child's name on his belongings, such as his coat, boots, and artwork. Allow the child to watch while the name is printed. Then he may like to try to copy his name, as his interest grows and his ability increases.

- Print names of objects in a room on paper signs and attach them to the objects. This action encourages the child to question signs and realize that letters can stand for objects and hold information.

- Keep paper and pencils near at hand so that signs can be incorporated by children into play as needed. For example, signs can be made to tell the names of block buildings. Signs may also be used to extend or enforce play. If a child is pretending to be a traffic policeman, ask him if he would like a sign that says *"Stop" and "Go."* Let the child make the sign and then, depending on the child's developmental level, print the words for the child or ask if he knows the letters. Or provide models of the words for the child to copy.

- Use a primary typewriter with large, clear type — or any typewriter — with a preschool child. Type a story as the child dictates.

Often the stories are very brief (a few words or a single sentence). If each story is typed on a separate sheet of paper, the child may then wish to illustrate it. Bound into a book, these pages preserve the story, which can be read again and again.

- Make charts for cooking projects. The charts have pictures and words telling what to do. For example: draw three eggs with the words "3 eggs" printed beside them. Show processes, as with a sketch of the eggs being broken. The child "reads" the recipe to find out what to do in the cooking process so he can complete the project with minimal help.

- Ask the child to help you make a shopping list. Tell the child the item needed such as bread and instruct the child to draw a picture of a loaf of bread. If the child knows that the word bread begins with the letter b, he can also write the first letter in the word.

- *Treasure-hunt walk.* Sketch pictures of objects that are found outside or paste actual objects on cards for the treasure hunt. For example, three red leaves or five short sticks are pasted on a card with the names of the objects printed beside the pictures: "3 red leaves" or "5 short sticks." The child goes on a treasure-hunt walk in which he attempts to find the objects his card pictures.

THE MECHANICS OF WRITING

Although handwriting is a developmental process, there are some skills that can help a child develop the physical readiness to write. The following activities help to develop eye-hand coordination and small-muscle skills:

- Encourage such activities as the use of clay, finger paints, easel paints and brushes, blocks, crayons, hammers and nails, puzzles, paste, and other media. They help the child develop eye-hand coordination and muscular control that are necessary for writing.

- Help the child, whenever he picks up a crayon, pencil, or felt-tip pen, to hold it in the proper relaxed position.

- Draw some dots on a large sheet of paper for the child to connect. Arrange the dots so they make a simple shape when connected, a shape such as a circle, square, or triangle. Show the child how to draw a line to connect the dots, and be sure to praise the child's work. A variation: Put dots on the paper in the outline of the child's name. Show the child how to connect the dots. If this seems too difficult, use just the first letter of the child's name.

- Encourage the child to freely explore cutting paper with the scissors. Show the child who can cut paper into different shapes: round, square, irregular, straight, zigzag, and curved. Some children do not have the small-muscle skills to cut shapes. Children who are too young to cut can be encouraged to tear paper.

- Show the child how to use the paper punch to make holes in paper. The circles punched out can be pasted onto colored paper to make a collage. The child may enjoy sewing through the holes using a large plastic needle threaded with yarn.

- Show the child how to use a stapler. Let the child staple strips of paper onto construction paper or to make anything he likes.

- String dyed macaroni. Pour ½ cup Isopropyl rubbing alcohol in a small container and add food coloring. (Water can be used instead of rubbing alcohol, but the color is not as bright. Supervise the activity closely because rubbing alcohol can be harmful if a child drinks it.) Add macaroni and stir until you have the desired shade. Drain the macaroni and place it on newspaper to dry. Have the child stir the macaroni as it dries to prevent its sticking to the newspaper. Show the child how to string the macaroni on a large needle threaded with fish line, dental floss, yarn, or string, to make necklaces or bracelets.

- Show the child how to make a paper fan by folding paper accordion-fashion. As the child folds, talk about words, such as "fold," "toward," and "away from." Let the child color the fan any way he likes.

- Give the child a large needle threaded with brightly colored yarn to weave back and forth between the ribs of a plastic produce box. (Cherry tomatoes and strawberries are sold in these boxes.)

- Show the child how to use the can opener and let the child help you open a can of peaches, pears, or mandarin oranges. Before opening the can ask the child to guess what is inside. Let the child eat the contents, as a snack.

- Show the child how to insert and turn a key in a lock. Talk about the key unlocking the door. Let the child try to open the door before and after it is unlocked.

- Build together with peas and toothpicks. Use dried peas that have been soaked overnight in water and drained, or use frozen peas that are slightly thawed. Show the child how to stick the toothpicks into the peas to connect the peas and toothpicks. Encourage the child to create any kind of structure he wishes. The structure dries in a day, and its parts can be painted and used as toys or as part of a mobile.

- Trace body parts. Instruct the child to trace around his hand and then around his foot. He may need help tracing around the toes and fingers. Write a statement under each picture, such as "This is Billy's hand" or "Joan traced around her foot."

- Allow the child to play freely with large nuts and bolts. Watch to see if the child knows how to unscrew the nut from the bolt. If necessary, show the child how. Later, show him the more difficult task of turning the nut onto the bolt.

- Show the child how to use a ruler as a guide to make a straight line. Other lines and shapes can be made by tracing around a jar lid or cookie cutter. Encourage the child to talk about the lines and shapes he makes.

- When the child is dressing, encourage him to practice zipping, snapping, and buttoning his clothes.

- Show the child how to drop clothespins into a milk carton with a wide opening.

- Let the child make a picture or collage out of beans, corn, macaroni, and scraps of material. These can be made on newspaper, paper grocery bags, or paper plates.

- Provide sets of alphabet letters in play materials. Letters that are made of materials such as wood, wood covered with sandpaper, or plastic are usually more interesting for the child to manipulate and more durable than those of paper or cardboard. The child can feel, look at, and arrange the letters. For example, the child who does not have the motor control necessary for writing letters can often perceive the shapes and thus can "write" words, such as his name, with block letters.

- If the child is eager to begin writing letters, you need not teach him the letters in alphabetic order. Start with the letters that are the easiest to make, then go to the harder ones. Here is one possible order you might want to use in teaching him the capital letters: I, L, X, T, H, F, E, A, M, V, N, P, U, C, W, O, Q, D, Y, Z, B, K, J, R, S, G. Remember, though, that this order may not be the order that is easiest for your child. It takes a child some time to learn to print these letters. Be patient, show him how to make the strokes that make up each letter, and give him lots of time to learn.

literature

*The worth of a book is what you carry away
from it.*
James Bryce

All great literature develops out of rich, sensory experiencing, powerful feeling, and deep thinking. It widens the child's sensitivity to expression and lets him see through the discerning eyes of the poet or storyteller. Life acquires a fuller and richer meaning as the child grows in his ability to identify himself vicariously with the lives of other people. Vivid life experiences are interpreted for him in a pattern of meaningful words. His natural enjoyment of rhythmic expressions, stories, and rhymes provides the simple but solid basis for his later esthetic development.

Their first contacts with literature provide mentally stimulating and emotionally satisfying experiences for children. Through books, stories, and verse, children are introduced to a world of beauty, imagination, and action with which they identify in terms of their past experiences. For many a child there is a pleasant surprise in the discovery that others have joys and sorrows, mishaps, and adventures akin to his own.

Taylor lists 15 purposes for using literature in the curriculum of the young child. These purposes summarize the values that literature can bring to a child's life.[6]

- To enrich or supplement first-hand experiences of the child
- To build correct concepts
- To clarify ideas
- To share experiences
- To build social relationships
- To foster appreciation of aesthetic things
- To present information
- To provide literary experiences through a variety of ways, such as poetry, information, nature, inspiration, everyday living, and holiday fun — also, to stimulate creative expression.
- To encourage verbal communication with other children and adults.
- To provide a period of quiet activity, a change of pace, or repetition of an enjoyable book.
- For the enjoyment which stories provide
- To acquaint the child with another way of learning about his world
- To stimulate new ideas
- To encourage good reading habits
- To care for the property of others

In exploring the field of literature for young children, you can make a good beginning with picture books. A picture book is one in which as much space is given to the picture as to the text and in which the story is evident from the pictures. The ideal picture book is one in which the text, illustrations, and format are

[6]Barbara J. Taylor, *A Child Goes Forth* rev. ed., (Provo, Utah: Brigham Young University Press, 1975), p. 78.

unified. Fine illustrations build good taste in the young child. The illustrations train his eye to appreciate color, line, and harmony.

There is an enormous selection of children's books available today. Some are clearly marked for preschool children, but others are not marked at all. So how do you go about deciding whether a book is suitable for your preschool child, both in age level and in subject matter? The question becomes one of choosing the right books; although there are many wonderful books written for children of this age, there are also many that are worthless. Here are some general criteria for choosing books for preschool children, as well as some specific suggested subjects:

Style. The style should be clear and simple, with short sentences and not too many unfamiliar words. Taking into consideration young children's short attention span, you should select a book that is not too long.

Content. Understandable, concrete ideas should be presented. One main character with a simple story line is generally best. The story should involve action and have a clear-cut ending. Some familiar details, recognizable people, animals, relationships, and feelings in realistic stories — as well as fantasy — capture the young child's interest.

Theme. Young children like books about familiar experiences, animals, families, and feelings common to young children. They like books about transportaion, machines, changing weather, growing things, seasons, humor, and people they know: policemen, firemen, mailmen, and storekeepers. Avoid books with themes that disturb preschoolers: abandonment or rejection by parents or key adults, frightening punishments, injury to the body, or other upsetting concepts.

Illustrations. For preschool children, at least, the illustrations are as important as the contents and theme. The illustrations should be numerous — one illustration for each important idea in the story. The illustrations must be accurate and synchronized. Children prefer illustrations that are clearn and easily recognizable for what they are, with true, realistic colors, if colors are used.

The illustrations should add something to the story, either with touches of whimsey or extra details.

How a book is read to a child can make a difference in how the child accepts and enjoys the story. The adult should sit at the child's level. If you are righthanded, hold the book level with the right shoulder. Tilt the book slightly down so it faces the child. Be sure the child can see the book. The reader's voice is a good tool to hold the child's attention. The voice can be varied from loud to soft to build a feeling of suspense. Questions might be asked, such as "Can you find the pink flower with your eyes?" Be familiar with the book and ad-lib if the child cannot hold his attention on the complete text of the book.

Children find enjoyment in the music of literature and poetry. Poetry stirs the imagination; it makes an emotional appeal. It is a joyous experience, and like other forms of literature, it can lead to creative expression for the child. Young children have a very basic enjoyment of the repetitions, alliterations, and rhythmic patterns of poetry. Without the slightest encouragement, they learn poetry by heart and proudly recite it to any willing listener. Unlike stories, which are usually reserved for a special storytime, poetry is best introduced in short doses at odd moments when it is suddenly appropriate: Read "The Swing," for instance, after the child has been swinging, or "The Fog" on a foggy day, and so on.

Following are a few suggested activities for developing an interest in and an enjoyment of literature.

literature activities

PRE-STORY ACTIVITIES

Appropriate activities can help to lead into the story and add interest to the story.

- Most children enjoy singing simple songs. Choose songs that deal with familiar experiences of children and that are preferably related to the story.

- Children enjoy doing as well as seeing and hearing. Finger plays can be used to lead into a story, but they should be short and of interest to the child.

- Music can relax the child and help him prepare for the story. Introduce the child to some of the good classical compositions and call them by name, but be sure the experience is not too long. When possible, correlate the mood of the music with the theme of the story.

- Pictures make good introductions to a story. But select with care the pictures you use with children. They should be simple illustrations so as to avoid confusion and distraction. A picture can stimulate responses if questions are asked: "What do you think these children are doing?" "Would you like to do this?" "Why do you suppose this child is happy?"

STORIES

There are many ways of telling stories or reporting on stories that are read.

- While you tell or read a story, draw crude stick figures and animals on a blackboard or a piece of colored paper. As the plot develops, let the child give you ideas for what to draw or let him draw the main characters. A variation: Let the child make up a story while you illustrate it on the board as he tells it to you.

- During stories with action, let the child go through movements that are indicated in the story.

- Sack, finger, or stick puppets may be used during the story. Often only one puppet (the main character) is all that is necessary to hold the attention of the child and make the story more enjoyable.

- Many stories can be told with the use of a flannel board and a few simple figures.

- Children delight in hearing stories told well. You or a child can retell a story just heard or a favorite story. Retelling not only allows for better eye contact, but it also gives the child an opportunity to form his own images of the story in his mind (mind pictures). Thus he need not rely constantly on an illustrator's interpretation.

- The child might tell about his favorite character in the story, in response to a question: "What was he or she like?"

- The child might tell the most exciting or interesting part of the story. You might then go back and reread that part of the story.

- The child can make a series of pictures or a hand-rolled movie of the storybook you have read.

- The child can pretend to be a book and tell what he holds within his pages.

- The child might put himself into the story discussing various ideas or events in the story as if he were there. For example: "If you were a circus pony, what adventure might you have?" or "If you were a dog that liked to run away, what might happen to you?"

- The child might make up his own book. The child makes a series of illustrations and you then print or type the dictated story a few lines on each page to correlate with the pictures. The child can make a cover for the book, and you can place the book on a special shelf to be shared with friends when they come to call. Some ideas for original stories follow:

  — One day I met a boy called _____. (Complete the sentence.) He was walking with a friend who was _____. They were playing_____, when all at once_____.

  — I am a boy. My name is *(child's name)*. I want a bicycle. (Complete the story by telling how this boy got the bicycle.)

  — Begin with a little idea and then blow it up: "I was angry at my mother so I ran away and_____!" or "I had a birthday party and_____!" or "I caught a yellow butterfly and_____!"

  — Use true ideas and retell events that really happened: "When I was small I did some funny things_____." or "We went on a long trip_____" or "My pet had a real adventure_____."

- Let the child practice telling the truth. After reading a story to the child, make statements such as, "The boy was very sad in the story." The child can then say yes or no, or turn his thumbs up for yes or down for no, depending on whether the statement is true or false.
- Add-on stories are fun for children. The adult might begin to tell a familiar story or a made-up story. The child then completes the story with either the correct ending or a made-up ending.

POETRY

"Oh, what a lovely thing to see a poem born and made, and hear it rhyme and sing" (author unknown). Children do love poems.

Nursery rhymes are an excellent introduction to poetry. Fortunately, there are many colorfully illustrated books to choose from. Most nursery rhymes have traditional tunes that the child may already know. Indeed, the child who has learned to sing a great many nursery rhymes invariably has a more musical approach to spoken poetry than the child without this background. The child who has sung nursery rhymes will say the lines of poetry with greater inflection, emphasizing the rhymes and raising and lowering his voice appropriately, just as he does when he sings the nursery rhymes.

- Make up jingles and rhymes anytime during the day when the occasion arises. Jingles are word-tinglers: "Taffy is laughy" or "Mrs. Morgan plays the organ." Begin with a line, and then let the child add his ideas: "I have a frog that is green. Some people think that he is_____."
- Finger plays invite active participation. The child can make up new lines to familiar finger plays.
- Record the child's poems on a tape recorder.
- Place the child's favorite poems or his original poems in a scrapbook.

- Make a poem tree. Hang the child's favorite poems on a twig that has been secured in a pot. Add new poems often to the poem tree.

6
creative
expression

No matter where the body is, the mind is free to go elsewhere.
W. H. Davis

many parents are not certain as to what creative expression really is or is not. Taylor states, "To some, creativity is linked strictly with the actual use of materials as paint or clay. This assumption of course, is erroneous. A child may express his innermost thoughts in other ways as well."[1] If this is true, creativity can be defined in many ways. Creativity can refer to the very young child, in that he is seeking to find out about his world, to explore, to discover, to make something new, to invent, and to shape — and he does this in his own creative way.[2]

Creativity, like other attributes, is a developmental process. Parents must provide opportunities and situations for creative expression:

> The creative being does not emerge suddenly. He develops gradually and grows as he faces problems and situations, recognizes them, and is able to solve or face them successfully. Experiences in art and music as well as in other activities . . . can contribute to the development of a creative individual.[3]

What shall parents do to nurture creativity in their children? Logan gives the following advice:

> Not give out ideas ready-made, certainly, but help each child realize the tremendous possibilities that lie within him. Children cannot create in a vacuum. Creativity emerges from rich experiences, from feelings, ideas, reactions and observations, from an atmosphere of freedom, encouragement, and appreciation, from the experiments a child makes.[4]

---

[1]Barbara J. Taylor, *A Child Goes Forth,* rev. ed. (Provo, Utah: Brigham Young University Press, 1975), p. 31.

[2]S. H. Leeper, R. J. Dales, D. S. Skipper, and R. L. Witherspoon, *Good Schools for Young Children: A Guide for Working with Three, Four, and Five Year Old Children* (New York: Macmillan, 1968), p. 337.

[3]Ibid

[4]Lillian M. Logan, *Teaching the Young Child: Methods of Preschool and Primary Education* (Boston: Houghton Mifflin Co., 1960), p. 308.

The parent-teacher who is convinced that the aim of education is the fullest possible development of each child's potential must consider the interests of the child, because in such interest lies the key to his capacities, talents, and achievements. Capacities are innate, but education can stimulate and encourage growth; it can guide the child by understanding the media in which he chooses to express himself; and it can give him opportunity, materials, and time to develop his capacities.

Creative expression needs protection as well as encouragement and stimulation. Young children express themselves in many forms, but, regardless of the form, they reveal all of themselves in every moment. Often, of course, these expressions do not emerge in the form an adult may desire. But if creativity is suppressed or if a child's efforts are compared with those of other children, the spark of genius may be lost. Encouragement must be given until a child builds confidence in his own style of expression. At the same time an adult can give help on techniques as help is requested.[5]

[5]Ibid., p. 309.

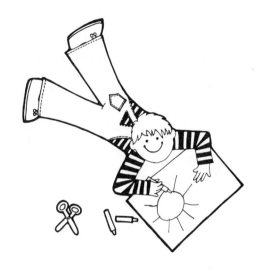

art

Drawing is easy. You just think your thought and draw your think.

A child

The child is an artist. He expresses not only what he feels but what he believes. Art experiences provide the opportunity for the child to use self-expression in visual form. This type of activity also provides the child with a way to express emotions that might otherwise be unacceptable, that is, it has therapeutic value. Art experiences can help the child guide his feelings into acceptable channels.

Logan suggests the following stages of artistic development in children:

The Age of the Scribbler. Sometime between the age of two and four most children have their first adventure in creating art: they scribble. The first scribbles are as definitely related to painting and drawing as the first babbling sounds are to speech. A simple "Tell me about your picture" may handle the situation. Easel paints are welcomed by children in the scribbling stage; so are blackboards and Plasticine.

In Search of a Symbol.   The five-year-old, as he paints away, is so intent on the work of the moment that he is scarcely aware of others around him. He is in search of symbols. He paints with deliberation, unhesitatingly, and without hurry. He often surveys his product with satisfaction.

The Symbol Is Found.   Beginning somewhere around age five is the schematic or symbolic stage. Two characteristics of this level of development are: the use of standardized formula for presenting the human figure, and the use of a baseline to indicate space relationships between objects in a picture. Having found his own formula, the child repeats it many times with evident satisfaction and delight. This formula expresses his concept of a human being in a way that temporarily satisfies him. It is important to realize that the child continues to paint his symbol until he has had an experience that jolts him away of it. At this point he should be encouraged. Simple comments from the adult can be very effective in encouraging the dubious beginner: "I like the way you put that shape next to that other thin shape." "My goodness, you have good ideas." "It is hard to make those two pieces of cardboard stick together, but you did it." The adult who is accepting of "your picture," "your idea" is accepting of you.[6]

Art is important because it enables the child to resolve, examine, and clarify ideas and concepts about which he is learning; at the same time he enjoys the freedom and independence of expressing original ideas. The child can also gain confidence in his own resources and realize that he is accepted as a unique and valuable person.

Children's art ideas are often predetermined by adults. Such predetermined outcomes rob the child of the opportunity to express his own creativity, and thus most of the values of art mentioned in the preceding paragraph are lost. Dictated art—coloring books, mimeographed forms of animals or people, follow-the-directions lessons with a step-by-step process providing the child with a product identical to another's, and demonstrations by the adult of how to draw an object or an idea—is detrimental to creative thinking and tends to make the child dependent upon adults for inspiration. The child thus becomes dissatisfied with his own

[6]Logan, *Teaching the Young Child,* p. 353.

attempts at creativity. The following concepts should be foremost in the parent's mind when the child is having an art experience:

- Try not to indicate a definite preference for work that looks like something specific. Representationalism is not requisite to art experience.
- No matter how minimal growth may seem, be sure to develop self-confidence and provide incentive.
- Keep competition out of the picture. Art is a personal, individual thing. Do not fail to recognize the child's attempts and display them in important places.
- Provide a variety of materials to sustain interest, and offer maximum opportunities for growth.
- When a material is new and exciting, do not impose a specific limitation about how it should be used. Let the child investigate it on his own.
- Remember that the highly creative child is the one who is most likely to deviate from what you expect him to do. Give him the opportunity to express his own ideas.
- Show the child reproductions and pictures of adult art. Encourage him to express his responses and feelings to them. Communicate that there is no one way that is right when making a picture, and that the way colors, lines, and shapes make us feel is important.
- Do not use patterns. Patterns are in opposition to all the values inherent in creative teaching. Patterns belong in mathematics.
- Have a wonderful time! Art is an exciting aspect of working with your child. It offers the adult the opportunity to share the child's feelings and reactions to the world about him.

The time to give a child help is when he asks for it and not before. Undue emphasis on technique at this early state is not warranted. The greatest contribution the parent can make to the child is to put up his picture for everyone to see. Let him realize that he is an artist and that he has ideas worth expressing and sharing. When a child asks for help, guide his conceptual understanding, not his hand. If you make the picture, it is your picture, not your child's. You should want to see the child's picture the way he thinks of it. If the child is too insecure to start, urge him to just make one part, maybe the head; then praise his results, no matter how meager. Encourage him onward.

art
activities

ENCOURAGING CREATIVE
THINKING IN ART

Help the child to think of new ideas to create.

- Say to the child, "If you could invent a new means of transportation, what would it be? Draw or construct how it would look."
- Ask the child, "If you had a funny-shaped piece of paper, what kind of an animal or automobile or house could you make it into?"
- Ask, "How do you think the world would look to a giant? Draw a picture of it."
- Ask, "What could you do with this empty box, this stick, this cardboard (beautiful junk)? How could you place it or arrange it to make something that's your very own idea?"
- Relate topics given to the child to either his actual personal involvement or his prior study and experience. Take your cues from the child's world. Typical subjects to suggest to him might include:

  — Your house
  — Your family
  — Where you like to play
  — Your favorite play thing to play with
  — An animal you know
  — How you feel when you're lonely
  — A make-believe place
  — What you want to be when you grow up
  — Clothes you like to wear
  — How you help others in your family
  — What you like to do when it is hot
  — Your self-portrait
  — Things that scare you
  — A friend
  — Someone you love
  — A trip you have taken

APPROPRIATE ART MATERIALS

Let the materials suggest a use to the child. He does not always need to be told what to do with them. Regardless of how many media are available to the child, do not feel that he should be interested in all art media. Regardless of stimulation and regardless of suggestions, each child undoubtedly is going to prefer certain media over others. If we keep in mind that what is happening to the child as he uses a medium is more important than what he produces, then we are working in a creative manner with the child. Following are suggestions for stimulating the child's interest in a variety of media.

Crayons

In general, the younger the child, the larger the crayon. Encourage the child to use the sides of a crayon as well as the ends. Here are some crayon activities:

- Place a leaf under a paper with the vein side up. Cover with paper, and then, using the side of the crayon, rub over the paper. You will soon see a leaf print begin to appear. Caution: The child must keep the paper still and must use the side, not the end, of the crayon. A single color may be used or several colors can be superimposed on each other. Also, leaves may be superimposed. This activity can also be carried out with coins, string, pieces of paper, wire screening, and burlap.
- Color a piece of paper completely with light-colored crayon, then cover that colored surface with dark crayon. Scratch through the dark color to the light color with the edge of blunt scissors or a tongue depressor.
- Put a heavy layer of crayon color on construction paper. Wash over the paper with tempera or water colors.
- Murals can be made by very young children. Ask the child to color designs or pictures on long sheets of butcher paper. Tack the paper on a fence outside for display. The child can have his own art show by putting up several of his paintings.
- Let the child make a costume out of large paper sacks, with details of the costume colored on. The costume can be fringed

for Indian garb, streamlined for a spaceman's suit, or modified as the child desires.

- Allow plenty of opportunities for free expression. Paper of all sizes and shapes should be available to encourage variety.
- Put crayon shavings between the folds of a piece of paper. Place this paper between newspapers and apply a hot iron on top until the crayon has melted into a design.
- Melt small pieces of crayon in aluminum foil and formed into unusual shapes. This provides the child with a crayon of a new shape and combined colors.

Chalk

Fat, soft chalk of different colors mixes with ease and provides a grand beginning for free expression. Chalk discourages tight, inhibited work and makes free expression easy. Covering each piece of chalk with a piece of aluminum foil, leaving about half an inch of the chalk exposed, prevents smearing. It also prevents the transferring of colors from one piece of chalk to another while they are stored. A variation: Try wetting the paper, especially brown paper bags, and then applying dry chalk; the colors will be bright and almost fluorescent.

- If a slippery surface is desired, liquid starch may be applied to the paper before the dry chalk. There is less friction with starch, and the paper is less likely to tear.
- Soaking pieces of large chalk in sugar water (one part sugar and two parts water) for about 15 minutes and then using the chalk on dry paper, is another method of application. Sugar gives the chalk a shiny look when dry. Let the child experiment.

Felt-tip Pens

Children love them, supervision is generally needed. In most cases, they can be used like crayons, but put newspaper, oilcloth, or a cookie sheet underneath the drawing paper.

Paste

Many children enjoy the sensory activity of pasting. They want to smear it and mess around with it rather than use paste functionally. Tolerance is necessary. Although paste is adequate for most jobs, more expensive glue is necessary for securing three-dimensional construction work and working with tissue paper.

Homemade, No-cook Paste. This is not so sticky as boiled paste. Add water to a handful of flour, a little at a time, until gooey. It should be quite thick so it does not run all over the paper. Add a pinch of salt.

Boiled Paste. Make it by combining ½ cup flour and cold water until it is as thick as cream; boil slowly for five minutes while stirring. Cool and add a few drops of oil of wintergreen, to retard spoiling and give a pleasing odor. Store in a covered jar and refrigerate if possible.

Scissors

Please make sure they cut! There is nothing more frustrating than trying to learn with a pair that is too blunt. Provide learn-to-cut times for beginners, where the only aim is to snip a pile of scraps. Let the child paste his miscellaneous scraps down later. You might post the results of the child's cutting attempts with a big sign saying, "I am learning to cut!"

Tearing, Punching, and Stapling

Children love to just tear, punch, and staple. Keep a stack of old magazines and newspapers on hand for this purpose. If you do not have a paper punch or if the child is too young to use it, the child can use the handle of a wooden spoon to punch large holes in the paper.

- If a paper punch is used, save the circles that the child punches from white waxed paper and put them in a jar full of water. After you fasten the lid on tightly he can shake the jar and make a snowstorm inside.

- Give your child a variety of paper, such as smooth, bumpy, heavy, and tissue-thin, all in different colors. Then ask the child if he can tear a tiny shape, an enormous shape, a wide shape, and the like. Let the child paste or staple all of the interesting, ragged shapes on a long piece of paper for a big, colorful mural. Tape the mural on an empty wall for all to see.

Paper

Offer the child an opportunity to work with varied sizes and kinds, not only to motivate his interest but also to increase his vocabulary and general understanding. Ask the child, "Which one feels bumpy? Smooth? Slippery? Wiggly?" Available kinds of paper include:

- Printer's remnants (often high-quality paper, which the printer gives away).
- Newsprint (available in art stores).
- Large paper bags cut open.
- White butcher paper (especially good for finger painting).
- Wallpaper books. (Use the blank side for painting, the patterned side for pasting.)
- Brown wrapping paper.
- Shelf paper.
- Shirt cardboards.
- Paper plates.
- Construction paper.
- Metallic paper.
- Gummed colored paper.
- Cellophane.
- Sandpaper.
- Holiday wrapping paper.
- Waxed paper (scratch on it with toothpicks).

Poster or Tempera Paint

It is inexpensive and should not be diluted so much that it becomes too pallid and watery. Fruit-juice cans or baby-food jars can be used for individual colors. These containers fit nicely into cardboard soda-pop cartons holding 6 to 8 bottles and offer great flexibility of use and minimize spilling.

Easels. Although easels are fun to use when painting, they are not necessary. Working on a flat surface minimizes dripping and appeals to many children. Use newspaper or an old shower curtain under easels or on the floor. Be sure the paper is large enough to allow for sweeping motions as the child paints. Include the child in the clean-up process; this is an important part of his learning.

Ink Blots. Prefold paper and drop thick paint onto the open sheet from a tongue depressor or brush. Refold and open, again. Several colors may be used.

Wet Paper. Wet the paper with a sponge and then drop paint with a brush. Watch the drops spread into designs.

String Painting. Dip short lengths of string into bowls of paint, drop the string on paper, and remove string. Or fold the paper and then pull the string out while the paper is held shut with one hand.

Block Printing. Dip objects into bowls of paint and then press or rub the objects on paper. The objects may be spools, corks, sink stoppers, sponges, jar lids, small blocks, scrub brushes, potatoes cut into shapes, combs, Q-tips, or wads of paper.

Dry-powder Painting. Put dry-powder paint in dishes at the easel or on a table. Paint with wads of cotton, to give a soft effect.

Textured Paint. Mix textured substances with the paints for different effects, adding a little glue to ensure sticking. Some suggestions for substances: salt (which sparkles when dry), sand, fine sawdust, and coffee grounds.

Spatter Painting. For this, you need wire screens in frames, a toothbrush, a pan of thin paint, and a design cutout to set under the screen and on the paper. Objects may be paper silhouettes, leaves, cookie cutters, or combined keys, forks, spoons, scissors, and tongue depressors. When one color is dry, another may be used.

Fancy Paper.   Cut easel paper into unusual shapes to stimulate more elaborate design-painting on the child's part: circles, triangles, free forms, egg shapes, trees, houses, and the like.

Different Surfaces.   Paint on different surfaces: paper towels, colored construction paper, printed newsprint, cardboard boxes, egg cartons, wallpaper, dry-cleaning bags, wooden blocks, cloth, clay, dried dough, sea shells, stones, tree branches, paper bags, oilcloth, or pine cones.

Corrugated Paper.   Corrugated paper or board is exciting to paint because a child can watch the paint mix in the grooves to make new colors. Paint with red, yellow, and blue colors.

Window Painting.   Bon Ami or Glass Wax may be colored with dry paint powder and used to paint windows.

Soap Painting.   Whip soap powder with a little water and add dry paint powder; brush on colored or white paper. The paint is very stiff and conducive to making designs.

Detergent Paint.   Poster paint mixed with detergent can be used to paint on glazed paper, plastic, aluminum foil, and glass.

Mixing Colors.   A child can mix his own paints to be used at the table or easel. Put out colors in small amounts in paper cups or muffin tins and allow the child to mix them. Mixing primary colors teaches the composition of secondary ones. Mixing black or white with primary colors teaches pastel tints and grayed tones.

Water Painting.   Large brushes and small pails of water can be used to "paint" fences, walks, tricycles, sides of buildings, and cement.

Roll Painting.   Fill roll-on deodorant bottles with tempera paint — a thinner solution than used on an easel — and let the child roll them on paper.

Sand or Salt Painting.   Color sand or salt by mixing it with dry powdered tempera paint or by rubbing chalk over it. Apply paste to paper and sprinkle colored salt or sand on the paper. Shake off all that does not adhere to the paste.

Squeeze Bottles.   Put paint in a squeeze bottle and add a little liquid starch to prevent the paint from spilling out too quickly. Now hold the bottle above the paper and squeeze. Raise and lower the bottle to change the size of the paint drops. Try different bottles and colors. Place the tip of the bottle directly on the paper and move it around to make all kinds of lines.

Straw Painting.   Drop paint onto paper. Then produce designs by blowing through drinking straws at the paint drops.

Foot Painting.   If you feel ambitious, mix up some paint, set paper on the ground outside and let the child paint with his feet.

Sponge Painting.   Dip pieces of sponge into paint and then dab on white or colored paper.

Brushes

For the most part, it is best if brushes are not too large and full. Provide a few narrower ones for the times when a child needs one. It is advisable to supply a separate brush for each color, along with some extra brushes and empty jars to enable the child to mix new colors at will. This is part of the excitement of painting: Do not discourage it. Try Q-tips and throat swabs for variety. Allow the child to mix and smear colors on his paper, for he is investigating and discovering, as well as expending emotion. Let the child wash his brushes during clean-up, for this can be almost as much fun for him as painting.

Tapes

Cellophane, masking, vinyl, and holiday wrapping tapes probably should be dispensed by an adult.

Finger Painting

This is an important activity, which frees the child and encourages him to partake of sensory experiences. Demonstrate how you can utilize arms, elbows, backs and palms of hands, and twisted arms. First wet finger-painting paper or shelf paper, and place it on painting surface, shiny side up. Remove air bubbles. For the young child, homemade finger paint is less expensive and just as satisfactory as the commercial product.

Finger-paint Recipe #1

Mix instant chocolate pudding according to the directions on the package. Or use hand lotion on a cookie sheet to provide the experience of finger painting for a very young child.

Finger-paint Recipe #2

2 cups liquid starch
6 cups water
½ cup soap chips

Dissolve the soap chips in water until lumps disappear. Mix well with starch and add colored tempera paint.

Finger-paint Recipe #3

Blend wheat paste (ordinary wallpaper paste) into slightly warm water and stir. Pour into individual containers; add colored tempera paint.

- Finger painting may be done directly on the kitchen table or on a cookie sheet. Paint can be wiped off easily with a sponge by the child.
- Use waxed paper for a change, instead of regular finger-painting paper, because of its transparent quality. A combination of any liquid dishwashing detergent and a dark-colored tempera paint (one part paint, one part soap) can be brushed onto waxed paper. Cover the surface evenly so the painter can make a simple picture. Press hard with a brush until a clear design becomes tacky. Then press brilliantly colored tissue paper squares (4" × 4") gently into the soapy surface until the entire area is covered. When completely dry, the pictures can be turned over and held up to a window, so the colored tissue glows through the waxed paper.

Mono-printing.   Printing may be done on cookie sheets, clean plastic, glass, linoleum, or an appropriate table top. Finger-paint paper, butcher paper, or unprinted newsprint paper can also be used for this activity. First spread an ample amount of paint on the surface. Proceed as if finger painting, with fists, hands, and fingers. In making a design, it is necessary to press hard so that the shiny surface can be seen. When the design is complete, place the paper carefully down on top and gently smooth the paper down with the palm of the hand so all areas of the paper are brought into contact with the paint; then slowly pull the paper up. The design on the paper is in reverse of what is on the surface.

Bathtub Painting.   Some children have fun finger painting with soap suds in the bathtub.

Foot Painting.   Use finger paints and large pieces of butcher paper for foot painting. This activity is especially good in summertime when it can be done outside.

Stickers and Gummed Materials

All gummed materials, such as labels, airmail stickers, reinforcements, colored dots, book-club stamps, stars, letters, paper strips, numbers, and seals can be used with a variety of paper. The child may choose to use them as parts of objects or to organize them in a nonobjective manner. Organization (designing and composing) is the important aspect of this activity. Motor development is also furthered.

Collage

Linear, three-dimensional materials can be pasted down to create fascinating pictures. These may be used in conjunction with crayons or paints. Combine articles of different textures (smooth, rough, crinkly, fluffy, or scratchy). Language growth is developed through discussion and expression of how it feels. Encourage your child to talk about which colors and textures he likes together and which color background paper seems best. You need strong glue, scissors, background paper, and an assortment of challenging collage materials, such as these suggested here:

TEXTURED MATERIALS

- Fur scraps
- Leather
- Seeds, popcorn
- Twigs

- Felt
- Burlap or sacking
- Corrugated paper
- Egg carton dividers
- Sandpaper
- Velvet
- Crackers
- Raisins
- Dry, puffed cereal
- Dried flowers
- Pebbles
- Feathers
- Cotton
- Pipe cleaners
- Shells
- Small wood chips
- Dry macaroni
- Leaves
- Dried beans
- Egg shells

PATTERNED MATERIALS

- Wallpaper samples
- Magazines and newspapers
- Printed percales
- Greeting cards
- Catalogs
- Patterned gift wrappings
- Rickrack
- Lace remnants

TRANSPARENT AND SEMITRANSPARENT MATERIALS

- Net fruit sacks
- Nylon net
- Lace
- Organdy
- Veiling
- Thin tissue paper
- Metal screening
- Colored cellophane
- Paper lace doilies

COLORED AND SHINY MATERIALS

- Sequins
- Glitter
- Aluminum foil
- Ribbon
- Christmas wrapping paper
- Metallic paper
- Paper from greeting cards
- Christmas tinsel
- Mica snow

SHAPES

- Buttons
- Drinking straws
- Wooden applicators
- Spools
- Scrap sponge
- Paper clips
- Cork
- Bottle caps
- Styrofoam
- Cupcake cups
- Heavy cotton rug yarn
- Macaroni, spaghetti
- Rubber bands
- Toothpicks
- Beads
- Fluted candy cups
- String
- Gummed stickers
- Tongue depressors

SCATTERING MATERIALS

- Sand
- Sawdust
- Tiny pebbles
- Shavings
- Twigs
- Salt
- Rice

Note: To color rice or macaroni, put 2 tablespoons rubbing alcohol and food coloring into a jar. Cap and shake well. Add rice and macaroni and shake again. Turn out onto paper towels and let dry approximately 10 to 15 minutes.

Sculpture

Working with clay and modeling media of all descriptions is a meaningful occupation for children, simply from the standpoint of sensory and manipulative satisfaction.

- You may obtain clay from a river bank or purchase it in powdered or moistened form. Its unique feature is that is hardens. (Plasticine, which has an oil base and usually does not harden, is usually not so popular with children.) Keep the clay balls covered with a damp cloth in a closed container when not in use. Children seem most creative when given clay and their own two hands, but they may also use tools, such as tongue depressors, Q-tips, rolling pins, cookie cutters, dull knives, and forks and spoons.

- Other sculpturing media can be made at home with either of the following recipes:

Uncooked Dough

Mix and knead 1 cup salt, 1½ cups flour, ½ cup water, 2 tablespoons oil. Use more flour to avoid stickiness, if necessary. Add food coloring if you wish. Store in a covered jar or a plastic bag in a refrigerator.

Cooked Dough

Mix together 1 cup salt, ½ cup cornstarch, and ⅔ cup water. Cook and stir constantly until the mixture thickens. Remove from heat and cool. Knead in vegetable coloring. Store in a refrigerator.

- Use potatoes, straw, toothpicks, wire, yarn, pipe cleaners, paper nut cups, and anything else you can think of to add to the sculpture. Encourage the child to be resourceful in figuring out how to affix and organize objects with his clay.
- Wire, for example, as electrician's wire (plastic-coated in bright colors), is available in hardware stores. Other spooled wires of narrow gauge are excellent for sculpture. Utilize scraps of wood for a simple base. Staples secure the wire.

Construction Activities

Carpentry and construction of puppets is discussed in "Role of Play."

VALUES OF SPECIFIC ACTIVITIES FOR PRESCHOOLERS*

ACTIVITIES \ VALUES	SENSORY EXPERIENCE	EXPLORATION	SATISFACTION & ENJOYMENT	SELF-EXPRESSION	MANIPULATION	EMOTIONAL RELEASE	EXERCISE IMAGINATION & INITIATIVE	GOOD WORK HABITS	LEARNING EXPERIENCE	SKILL & CONCENTRATION	EYE-HAND COORDINATION	HARMONY, RHYTHM & BALANCE	INSIGHT INTO OWN FEELINGS	DEVELOPS LARGE MUSCLES	DEVELOPS SMALL MUSCLES
BLOCKS		•	•	●	•	●	•	•	•	●	•	●	•	●	
CHALK	•	•	•	•	•	•	•	•	•	•	•	•	•	•	•
CLAY	●	•	•	●	•	●	•	•	•	•	•	•	●	•	•
COLLAGE	●	●	•	•	•	•	●	•	•	•	•	•	•		•
CRAYONS	•	•	•	•		•	•	•	•	•	•	•	•		•
CUTTING & PASTING	•	•	•	•	●	•	•	•	•	•	•	●	•	•	●
DOMESTIC AREA	•	●	•	•		●	●	●	•	•		•	●		•
PAINTING Easel	•	•	•	●	•	●	●	•	•	•	•	•	●	•	
PAINTING Finger	●	•	●	●	●	●	•	●	•	•	●	•	●	•	
SAND	•	•	•	•	●	•	•	•	•	•	•		•	•	•
STRINGING	•	•	•	•	•		•	•	•	•	●		•		•
WATER	•	•	•	•	●	●	•	●	•	•	•	•	•		•
WOODWORKING	●	•	•	●	•	●	●	●	•	•	●	•	•	●	•

*Taylor, *A Child Goes Forth*, p. 39.

NOTE: The larger dots indicate greater value for activity.

music

What will a child learn sooner than a song?
Alexander Pope

Music is one of the vital human experiences in the lives of children. It is not yet the skill based upon abstract patterns that perhaps it will become later. Music is just one more way for a pre-school child to express himself creatively.

Over emphasis should be on the growing, active, creative child; his enthusiasm for life and his natural inclination to respond to music are the important factors. There is warmth, energy, and potential power for creative growth as the child, without concern for technical perfection or mechanics of performance, expresses his own feelings through song.

Children should sing 10 times as much as is now the custom,

just as they should talk 10 times as much as now is permitted. A variety of spontaneous musical activities lays the foundation for a well-rounded experience in music.[7]

Although some children have the ability to reproduce a tone carefully, many children sing with more enthusiasm than quality. Do not be discouraged if a child's voice is not high, sweet, and melodic. Musical experiences can help improve the child's voice; however, the main concern is that the child might enjoy music and that he might have opportunities to sing, listen, and appreciate songs.

The following suggestions will help to encourage spontaneous musical experiences:

music activities

VOCAL ACTIVITIES

Children enjoy listening to the sound of their own voices, and they develop appreciation for music through these activities.

- Singing nursery rhymes or familiar songs, teaching new songs, encouraging him to sing while he builds with blocks or carry on other work activities, playing folk songs on a recorder while the child sings along, and allowing the child to hum tunes help a child discover his singing voice.
- Recording the child's singing and then playing it back to him can be great fun for the child and helps the child to hear his own voice as others hear it.

[7]Logan, *Teaching the Young Child,* pp. 323-24.

COMPOSING SIMPLE SONGS

Children love to make up words to go with melodies they know, and they find pleasure in experimenting with words and melodies.

- Help the child by encouragement to compose original words to known melodies.
- Encourage the child to sing original melodies to known words.
- Let the child make up original words and original melodies.
- Together with the child, make up new verses to an old song.
- Sing to the child, using first and last names or nicknames, such as "Mary Douglas, how are you? Hallelujah." "Susie Smith, touch your eyes. Hallelujah." "Honey loves to dance. Hallelujah." Encourage the child to make up songs about members of the family.

LISTENING TO MUSIC

Children enjoy listening to quiet music played in the background during an art period or when they are tired or irritated. Listening to music can stimulate creativity.

- Play a tone-matching game with the child. The child echoes tones the adult sings or plays on an instrument.
- Give the child a reason for listening. Help him listen for visual images and ideas brought to mind — and to follow the melody and hear different instruments.
- Ask the child what the music says to him.
- When a child is resting, instruct him to close his eyes and see what pictures he can envision as the music is played. After the rest, discuss the child's mind-pictures and perhaps write down what the child says. Or let the child draw what he envisioned.

- Ask the child to listen to familiar songs played or hummed. Then ask the child to identify the song.

- Help the child to become aware of musical characteristics. When a child does what the music tells him to do, such as tapping, clapping, and jumping, he starts to listen for fast-slow or loud-soft qualities of music as well as for various rhythm combinations. In a way, the child becomes aware of the counting value of different kinds of notes.

- Teach the child to identify instruments and sounds. A child enjoys seeing pictures of many instruments he has heard. He can try to listen for a trumpet or violin on a record and then match the sounds of the more easily recognizable instruments with their pictures.

- Allow the child to find out that there are many ways to make sounds with any instrument. With free access to drums, the child can learn that a drum sounds different when struck in the middle than at the edges and that it sounds different if hit by a soft-headed stick, a plain stick, a whisk, or a hand. Give free access to all kinds of instruments, even homemade ones.

- Pick out simple tunes with one finger on the piano, and then show the child how to do this. The child delights in being able to play a few familiar notes. Other instruments may also be used to play the familiar tunes.

- Collect bottles with small openings, such as soda-pop bottles, and bottles with large openings, such as quart jars. Blow into the openings to demonstrate the different sounds that can be made with different-size bottles. Let the child listen for high and low sounds. Stand bottles with large openings on the table and tap gently with a spoon. Let the child explore the different sounds the bottles make by blowing into them and by tapping them with a spoon.

- Make music by plucking strings or rubber bands that have been stretched over a box with a hole in the top. Let the child pluck a string and talk about the sound it makes. Show the child a violin or pictures of stringed instruments, and talk about the music they make.

movement—rhythm and dance

Only by fostering and developing creative activities of mind and body . . . can we hope to renew the much-needed spiritual aspects of our life today.

Gertrude Johnson

Expression through spontaneous bodily activity is as natural to the child as is breathing. If this innate tendency is encouraged as the child develops, it provides an intensely satisfying way of expressing emotions in a creative art form and it can provide a reliable foundation for artistic expression in the dance. All children are creative, but they express this tendency in various ways. Few children are equally at home in all forms of the creative arts, and thus each child must be given an opportunity to experience a variety of creative forms in order to find the most satisfying means of self-expression.[8]

Creative rhythmic movement is the child's interpretation of ideas and feelings, which he expresses through the use of his body. Creativity, rhythm, and movement are the three constant elements, regardless of the terms used. Children discover that the body is an instrument and that movement is a medium of expression. They translate feelings, ideas, and thoughts into movement.

Creative rhythmic movement does not, any more than other art forms, take place in a vacuum. It requires the elements essential to any artistic expression: a permissive atmosphere, time to create, space, and guidance.

The purpose or value of a rhythm program is that it attempts to give a child the opportunity to:

• Experience the joy of expressing himself in another creative form.

• Develop motor coordination, posture, and poise.

• Alleviate general strain and tension and provide emotional release.

• Interpret his own impulses rather than imitate someone else's ideas and motions.

• Develop an appreciation of listening and expressing.

• Experiment with the piano, chimes, drums, sticks, bells, tambourines, and other instruments.[9]

The following activities will aid you in providing the child with creative expression in the form of rhythm and dance.

[8]Logan, *Teaching the Young Child*, p. 310.
[9]Logan, *Teaching the Young Child*, pp. 313–315.

movement
activities

EXPLORING BODY MOVEMENT

The body can express feelings and interpret the mood of the music.

- Introduce a few body movements, such as swinging, bouncing, and shaking. Then let the child explore the many possibilities of each. Periodically, while the child is doing free movement, ask him to freeze while you place a hand on his back or shoulder. Then tell the child to dance or move to express how your touch affected him.

- Instruct the child to act out the thing that most frightens or disturbs him. Ask him to act out imaginatively his resolving of that fear or disturbance.

- Ask the child to get into and out of an imaginary box or bag.

- Ask the child to explain in movement his ideas of different forms of transportation: boat, horse-drawn cart, plane, train, and the like.

- Instruct the child to lift heavy and light objects, and then in pantomime.

- Say, "See if you can move the very smallest part of your _____ Now move the largest part."

- Encourage the child to pretend he is walking in the following ways: as if in the rain, snow, or hot sun; as if he were late, had lots of time, or were with a friend; as some people walk — bumpily, smoothly, or cross-leggedly; like someone you know — mailman or grandma.

- Instruct the child to be a monster or a bug and then move only the ways that the bug or monster shape allows.

- Say, "See if you can move five different parts of your body, one right after another."

- Talk about all kinds of weather (snow, hail, heat, cold, rain) and ask the child to tell how he feels when he is exposed to them. Next tell the child to act out and show in movement the way he feels about each.

- Ask the child to do a specific locomotor movement. Tell the child to get as close to something or someone as possible, but without touching it or him.

- Direct the child to pantomime an activity such as going on a hike:

  - "Decide what to take."
  - "Roll a pack; tie it; put it on your back."
  - "Walk fast, slow, up hills, down hills."
  - "It is rest time; take off the pack; relax."
  - "Put up your tent; hammer in stakes; set up poles; pull it up."
  - "Make a fire with paper, sticks, and logs; strike a match; blow."
  - "Cook steaks, hot dogs, and marshmallows."

- *Silly Putty.*   Show the child the many things that the putty can do: stretch, bounce, wiggle, stick, shatter, break. Direct him to perform each movement as it is introduced.

- Place a few chairs around the room to help the child become aware of space. Ask the child to move from chair to chair, improvising on each. He might try balancing on them, taking the shape of a chair, or jumping off a chair.

- Instruct him to perform movements with balloons to suggest the following: Stretching a balloon, blowing it up, letting the air out all at once, squeeking it, rubbing the balloon to make it cling to something, squeezing one end to make the other end bigger, and popping the balloon. Use balloons first to show all these things before the child does the movements. Also pretend to be holding helium balloons.

- Relaxation. Show the child a rag doll; show that it has no bones and that it sits and falls limply. Ask the child to imitate the doll. Next instruct the child to lie on the floor and be very limp. Check the limpness by moving his head back and forth and by lifting his arms and legs and letting them fall.

- Tension. Give the child an elastic band. Tell him to place it over his five fingers, stretch it open, and notice the tension. Next let the child take the shape of the elastic when the elastic is dropped on the floor. Tell him to open his limbs with the same tension that the elastic had.

- Prompt the child to make the shape of numbers or letters with his body.

INTERPRETING RHYTHMS

All of life is composed of rhythms, but the child needs opportunities to discover and explore them.

- Use a rhythmic instrument to get movement initiated. Ask the child to respond to the sound as it is played louder, faster, and unevenly.

- Use the rhythms of the child's name and the names of family members. Clap the beat, chant the words, and discover the accent, where the clap is louder.

- Have the child pick a number between one and ten. Accent with a drum (or tapping on the table top) that count the child has selected as you count from one to ten.

- Play telegraph. Clap a rhythm and encourage the child to answer back with the same rhythm, either by tapping his foot, clapping his hands, or employing some other body movement.

- Ask the child to do various body movements involving a variety of rhythms:

  — Walking fast, very fast; with slow, heavy, and droopy steps; with long steps, tiny steps, on toes, on tip toes, on heels, and to drum beats.
  — Walk, run, and end with a jump.

— Walk, alternating fast and slow steps.

— Stamp your feet in loud and soft patterns.

— Stamp loudly and crashingly.

— Leap, skip, and then jump.

— Jump in one spot to the rhythm of the sound.

— March briskly and then skip lightly and softly.

- Help the child to see rhythm in the waving of trees, grass, plants, moving clouds, swaying branches, walking, dancing, repetition of patterns, and movements of the postman or policeman.

- Play musical games to tunes like "London Bridges," "Pop Goes the Weasel," "Farmer in the Dell," and "Skip to My Lou."

- Encourage the child to use gestures along with songs: Chug along like a train; zoom like an airplane; leap like a kangaroo or frog or rabbit; waddle like a duck.

- Teach the child to clap a motif, like long, short, long, long. Direct him to memorize it. Next tell him to skip, run, or hop around the room: At a signal—from piano, drum, or hand clap—he must stop and clap the motif.

- Instruct the child to gallop across the room while you clap. Clap softly when he gets far away and loudly when he comes closer. Change places with the child.

- Suggest that the child perform movements to the following chants:

   — "Shake your head, shake your head, shake your head like it's full of lead."

   — "Bounce your shoulders, like they're two big boulders."

   — "Shake your knees like they're a breeze."

   — "Swing your arms; it will do no harm."

   — "Swing your hip and make it flip."

   — "Pace in place like you're in a race."

   — "Bend your back like you've got a pack."

—"Prance and prance like there's ants in your pants."
(Do each one twice.)

PLAYING SIMPLE INSTRUMENTS

The child needs an opportunity to produce simple rhythms.

- Allow the child opportunities to experiment with and enjoy various rhythmic effects and different tones with drum, triangle, rattles, bells, piano, tambourine, and cymbals.
- Try out percussion instruments to see which is best to accompany a song you are going to sing. Let the child help you decide.
- Make simple rhythmic instruments from items found around the home. Allow your child to do the same.

—*Pot Lids.* Two flat lids make a pair of cymbals.

—*Salt Boxes.* Fill each with a handful of rice or pebbles to make a rattle or maraca. (Tape the opening in the lid securely to prevent spillage.)

—*Oatmeal Boxes.* They become drums and tambourines. Tape the lid onto the carton and shake the whole thing, or use the lid for a tambourine.

—*Hair Combs.* Cover them with toilet tissue to produce harmonicas; they have a nice brassy sound. Show the child how to hold the tissue-covered comb against his mouth and sing or hum with his mouth slightly open. (It does not tickle that way.)

—*Shoe Box.* Take the lid off and stretch eight to ten rubber bands of different sizes around it to make a harp or a guitar to be plucked.

—*Building Blocks.* Tack or glue sandpaper to one side of two wooden blocks. When they are rubbed together in time to music, the sandpaper produces a shuffling sound.

- Use brown paper bags to make hats for each band player, to add interest to the playing of musical instruments. Roll back the edges to make brims of different shapes.

7
the role
of play

Play is the child's work.
L. K. FRANK

ven today there appears to be some confusion about the value of play. Frank says, "Part of the confusion arises from the old distinction between work and play, with the feeling that, while work is good, play is somewhat questionable.[1] In order to clarify the meaning of play, we might examine various statements regarding this function.

Piaget makes this statement from his observations of children: ". . . Games (synonymous with play) reproduce what has struck the child or evoke what has pleased him or enabled him to be more fully part of his environment."[2] Frank states, "Play is the way the child learns what none can teach him. It is the way he explores and orients himself to the actual world of space and time, of things, animals, structures and people."[3] Play can be satisfying and pleasurable, and these are good desirable ends for young children. Scarfe considers play to be an educational process:

> A child's play is his way of exploring and experimenting while he builds up relations with the world and with himself. In play he is learning to learn. He is also discovering how to come to terms with the world, to cope with life's tasks, to master skills. In particular, he is learning how to gain confidence. In play a child is continually discovering himself anew.[4]

Other purposes and characteristics of a child's play are set forth by Leeper: "Play may serve as a means of helping the child to solve a problem, play is self-revealing, and repetition is an important aspect of children's play, as it helps the child consolidate his skills and become more expert at experimenting on his own."[5]

[1]L. K. Frank, "Introduction", in Ruth E. Hartly and R. M. Goldenson, *The Complete Book of Children's Play*, (New York: Thomas Y. Crowell, 1957), p. vii.

[2]J. Piaget, *Play, Dreams and Imitation in Childhood*, trans. Gattengo and Hodgson, (New York: W. W. Norton, 1962), p. 155.

[3]L. K. Frank, *The Complete Book of Children's Play*, p. viii.

[4]N. B. Scarfe, "Play is Education," in *Readings from Childhood Education*, (Washington, D.C.: ACEI, 1966), p. 357.

[5]S. H. Leeper, R. J. Dales, D. S. Skipper, and R. L. Witherspoon, *Good Schools for Young Children: A Guide for Working with Three, Four, and Five Year Old Children* (New York: Macmillan, 1968), p. 312.

A child's play behavior falls into six categories: Unoccupied, solitary, onlooker, parallel, associative, and cooperative. The sequence includes ages three through five years. However, each child progresses at his own rate through these stages. Yet he should occasionally be allowed to experience a variety of forms of play regardless of age. A child should also be given opportunities to participate in the following types of play: sensory-pleasure play, dramatic play, creative play, and skill-building play. The following sections will supply you with ideas for providing these opportunities for your child.

dramatic play

The goal [is] the understanding of the
larger physical and social environment,
and one's place in it.

Millie Almy

Dramatic play is spontaneous and free of adult direction or control. According to Greene and Petty, "In dramatic play, children identify themselves with persons or things with which they have had firsthand contact or about which they have learned vicariously."[6]

The parent's responsibility includes (1) providing many interesting opportunities for the child to experience life, since the child's creative efforts are limited to his experiences; and (2) providing space, materials, and time for the activity. Once this

[6]H. A. Greene and W. T. Petty, *Developing Language Skills in the Elementary School,* (Boston: Allyn and Bacon, 1959), p. 349.

has been done, usually nothing more is required. Dramatic play may take many forms. Possibilities include make-believe, acting out of stories, and puppet shows.

dramatic play activities

MAKE-BELIEVE PLAY

Often when a child plays at make-believe, he pretends to be someone he wants to understand better. He tries to find out what it is like to be a mommy, a daddy, a big sister, a fireman, or a policeman. By putting himself in the other person's shoes, he begins to find out what the other person's job is and how he feels.

Sometimes a child acts out his secret wishes. If he doesn't like being small for his age, he may pretend to be big. If his big brother bullies him, he can play big brother.

While he is pretending, he also learns to handle some of the negative feelings that are not approved by adults. Occasionally, he uses make-believe play to help get rid of anxieties brought on by scary stories and TV programs.

Props for Make-Believe Play

The more props a child has, the better his play can be. If you provide him with equipment used by the people he is playing, he can play the parts more thoroughly and understand them better. Props need not be new or correct to the last detail. Children's imaginations provide whatever is missing. By reorganizing and changing a few props, you can convert a room corner from one setting to another. Whatever kind of corner you have, there are some props that are essential and basic to all make-believe games:

Domestic Scenes

- *Women's Clothes.* Shoes, hats, scarves, gloves, veils, blouses, pocketbooks, costume jewelry (no pins), hair bands, wigs, skirts, and lengths of fabric.
- *Men's Clothes.* Shirts, hats and caps, shoes, clip-on ties, vests, scarves, and gloves.
- *For Bathing Babies.* Dolls, towels, plastic dishpan, soap, and baby powder.
- *For Washing and Ironing Clothes.* Clothes, tub, clothespins, clothesline, iron, and ironing board.
- *For Dressing and Caring for Baby.* Doll, bed, rocking chair, clothes, and stroller.
- *For Housecleaning.* Broom, dustpan, dustcloth, mop, and wastebasket.
- *For Baking and Preparing Meals.* Rolling pin, cookie cutters, dishes, pans, table and chairs, and play stove. (Dime stores carry good-quality aluminum pans that are much sturdier than the pieces in the toy cooking sets. Plastic dishes from a dime store are better than cheap toy sets).
- *For Telephoning.* *Two toy telephones.* (They encourage conversation and are appropriate to any situation.)
- *Other Items.* Hats of all kinds, eyeglass frames (without glass or plastic lenses), toolchest, lunch box, and briefcase.

Community Scenes

- *Doctor and Nurse.* Flashlight, cot and pillow, rags for bandages, tongue depressors, cotton balls, bandages strips, gauze, a nurse's hat, a used hypodermic syringe *without* the needle (from a doctor), and empty medicine vials. (Do not use hard candy as medicines, for too many children's medicines look like candy.) Do not buy a toy doctor's kit with plastic parts, which come apart or break easily. Instead, make your own by filling an old shaving kit or pocketbook with the items mentioned above. A real stethoscope, which is indestructible and which really works, can be purchased for a small sum.
- *Mailman.* Old letters, magazines, newspaper, boxes, string,

wrapping paper, tape, envelopes, paper (new or used), and trading stamps.

- *Grocer.* Paper bags, toy cash register, shelves, empty cans, food boxes and cartons, balance scale, apron, and either hand bell or buzzer. (A bell lets people in for a visit, calls a store clerk for service, or announces a fire to firemen.)
- *Teacher.* Chalk, chalkboard, books, paper, pencils, bell, and some stuffed dolls or animals for pupils.
- *Entertainer.* Records, record player, musical instruments, costumes, makeup.
- *Fireman.* Old hose, raincoat, boots, belt, big boxes, and step-ladder.
- *Indian, Cowboy, Clown, and Other Characters.* Costumes that may be left over from Halloween.
- *Other items.* Old sheets, blankets, or bedspread for draping over tables or chairs to make a tent, wigwam, house, or cave.

Transportation and Travel

- *Train.* Cardboard boxes or chairs, whistle, tickets, paper punch, pillows, and suitcase.
- *Airplane.* TV-dinner trays, magazines, tickets, luggage, belts on chairs, and goggles.
- *Spaceship.* Space food, space helmet (keg or ice cream carton), large cardboard box (for spaceship), gloves, snowsuits, and aluminum foil.
- *Bus.* Chairs with cord, coins, hat and coat for driver, step stool.
- *Boat.* Life jacket, inner tube, boards for oars, and wheel for steering.

Outings

- *Camping.* Tents, sleeping bag or bed roll, backpack, canteen, mess kit, hiking boots, flashlight, and cot.
- *Restaurant.* Tables, chairs, menus, dishes, aprons, pencils and writing pads, food, cash register, and trays.

MAKE-BELIEVE CORNERS

Household furnishings scaled down to size are the basics of a make-believe corner. Try to avoid the flimsy metal or plastic items so readily available. Many of the furnishings can be made by you or the child from cardboard boxes or wooden crates. Many of the props can be borrowed from your kitchen. Dress-up clothes and other small props may be kept in a box or drawer. But like all toys, they are better used if they are kept in a place that allows more organization and easy access.

How Can a Parent Help in Make-Believe Play?

Essentially adults provide the time, space, and some simple props for dramatic play to occur and then leave the rest up to the child. But there are a few things you can do to help the child along. Sometimes the game or pretend player starts well, but later falls apart. The child gradually loses interest and drifts away, because the child doesn't have enough facts to keep the pretend situation going. For example, in a game of fireman, the child may get bored with running back and forth to put out fires. When you see the game beginning to deteriorate, it is time to step in: "Firemen don't spend all their time fighting fires. They spend a lot of time at the firehouse. What do you think they do there?" The child may know, but if he does not, tell him, "They clean the firehouse; they wash and polish the trucks." Provide the child with rags or sponges to wipe down the trucks, and a small dish of polish to wax them. After an incident like this, it is time to visit or revisit the firehouse and to read a book like *Fireman Small*. By doing this you give the child more facts to incorporate into his make-believe play.

Even make-believe play that has little adult direction can help the child develop certain important concepts. Dressing in adult clothes helps the child clarify identities and sex roles. Children of three and four are full of misinformation and confused facts. You can overhear a great deal of this when you are observing

133

make-believe play. Sometimes when children are deeply involved in a game of make-believe, even a casual correction may interrupt the flow of the game. If that is the case, wait until later to correct the confusion.

ACTING OUT STORIES

Creative dramatic differs from make-believe play, in that the idea which is the point of departure is not completely original with the child. The best things to begin with are the child's favorite nursery rhymes, poems, stories, or songs. The ones you select should have simple plots that include movement.

After you have reread a familiar rhyme (or whatever you have selected), tell the child he will have a chance to do what the poem says. Repeat the verse, slowly and clearly, as the child pantomimes his role. Stories like *Goldilocks and the Three Bears, Are You My Mother?*, or *Caps for Sale* are natural for acting out because they are simple and involve action.

Acting out a trip that is planned in the near future can make the trip less awesome because a child will learn what to expect. The child can act out events such as taking a walk, getting ready to have a party, and having lunch at a restaurant.

Most children enjoy acting out the stories on records. *Peter and the Wolf* is an excellent record to pantomime. The background music adds much to the child's ability to be creative in his movements.

PUPPETS

Children enjoy puppets because they provide variety and because they put a little distance between the children and roles that are too frightening for them. The simplest hand and finger puppets are the best for play. Marionettes are too complicated for most children to manipulate.

Puppets Children Can Make

- *Filled Paper-Bag Puppets.* Give the child a brown-paper lunch bag, and instruct him to fill it out with wads of newspaper. (You may have to crumple the paper first.) When the bag is full, the child inserts a toilet-paper roll into the opening, while you close the bag around it with string or wire. The roll serves jointly as a neck for the puppet and a handle for the child. The child then paints or glues features on the puppet, or uses a combination of the two techniques.

- *Paper Bag Puppets.* Ask the child to draw a face on out side of a small lunch-size paper bag. The fold at the bottom of the sack becomes the mouth of the puppet. A hole can be made in the mouth fold for the child to stick his finger through, giving the puppet a tongue.

- *Old Sock and Old Mitten Puppets.* A child can slip his hand into the toe of his sock and make the puppet "talk" by moving his thumb up and down against his four fingers. You might sew two buttons on near the toe for eyes, another for the nose, and a slip of colored paper for the mouth.

- *Stick Puppets.* Once a child has begun to draw recognizable figures, he can make a very simple puppet by cutting out a figure he has drawn and gluing or stapling it onto a tongue depressor. A child can make another kind of stick puppet by pasting geometric shapes onto a tongue depressor to form human figures.

Puppets You Can Make

- *Darning-Egg Puppets.* Glue felt features on a darning egg. Use yarn or wood shavings for hair. Push the handle downward through a hole in a man's handkerchief (or a piece of fabric the same size) to serve as clothes for the puppet. The puppet is held and manipulated under the handkerchief.

- *Rubber-Ball Puppets.* Paint features on a small, hollow rubber ball. To manipulate it, the child pushes his index finger up through a hole cut in a man's handkerchief or piece of fabric and through a hole in the rubber ball.

- *Apple, Potato, or Carrot Puppets.* Cut facial features from felt and secure them on the fruit or vegetable with straight pins.

With an apple, remove parts of the core making a hole in the bottom big enough for a child's index finger. Manipulate this puppet just like the hollow-ball puppet.

- *Hand Puppet with Face.* On a piece of fabric, trace around your flat hand; second, third, and fourth fingers together, and thumb and pinkie out. Cut two pieces of fabric this shape and seam them together around the edge, leaving the bottom open. If you use felt, it does not need hemming; it is strong and the seams do not ravel. Use buttons for eyes and yarn for hair, and embroider a mouth or glue on a felt one.

Puppet Stages You Can Make

- A table lying on its side is the easiest puppet stage to prepare. The puppeteer hides behind the table, using the top of the table as the edge of the stage.
- An upright table, with a sheet taped to the front, hanging all the way to the floor, is another easy-to-make stage. The table top is used as the stage floor.
- A grocery box with the top and bottom flaps removed also becomes a puppet stage. Lay it on its side on a table so you can look through it. The puppets are manipulated at the back of the opening.
- A grocery box with both top flaps and one bottom flap removed can be made into a TV set. Tape the remaining flap in place, and attach buttons or bottle caps to it with paper fasteners to make the dials. You can attach a cloth at the rear for a backdrop.

Getting Started with Puppets

The young child is happy being a puppeteer for dolls, stuffed animals, or the simplest hand puppets. If you direct questions or conversations to these puppets, the child answers for them. You can plan an acting activity based on a story, rhyme, or poem that the child is familiar with. When you tell the child that it will be acted out, tell him that the puppets will be the actors.

And if you leave puppets on shelves or anyplace that they are easily accessible, the child will use them to produce impromptu puppet shows.

indoor and outdoor play

Work consists of whatever a body is obliged to do
and play consists of whatever a body is not obliged to do.

Mark Twain

Regardless of the activity, planned or unplanned, the child
has certain requirements for his play. Space, materials, and equipment are vital to the child's play, whether it be indoor or outdoor play.

Space is important to the development of a child: He needs
an opportunity to explore freely in ample space. Occasionally the
child should be allowed to organize his own space, even if only
by moving chairs to his liking.

A variety of materials should be provided. These are the media through which children develop physical strength and motor coordination, dramatic play, creative activities, and social skills. Materials should be available for both indoor and outdoor activities—and will be used creatively if they are made available in variety and abundance.

Equipment need not be expensive. Much of a child's play equipment can be gathered or made from free or inexpensive materials. But the equipment should suit the developmental stage of the child and not be too challenging to his physical strength or his motor coordination.

indoor- and outdoor-play activities

INDOOR PLAY EQUIPMENT

Felt Board and Felt Pieces. The child handles, feels, and arranges the precut shapes to form familiar objects or a pleasing design. A generous selection of felt or pellon pieces allows for different kinds of learning. The following are useful: geometric shapes (circles, squares, triangles, rectangles in different sizes and colors); numerals (0–10); objects for counting (10 of each object); alphabet symbols; animals (circus, zoo, farm, pet); people (community helpers, family); clock symbols (numerals, hands); and nursery-rhyme characters. Cut out pictures from magazines and paste to felt-backed paper to be used to illustrate a favorite story or poem.

Pegboard. These are generally thought of for use in teaching a child to count, but the placing and arranging of pegs intrigue the child before actual counting begins. The board has 100 peg holes; the child inserts the colored pegs until all the holes are filled or until he decides he has done enough. Designs and scenes can be created.

Puzzles.   Puzzles provide a valuable means of developing hand-eye coordination. In addition, they demonstrate, in a memorable way that a whole is made up of parts. For this reason, each piece of a beginning puzzle should be cut out realistically to represent an object. Beginning puzzles should have no more than eight to ten parts; too many pieces cause frustration. As the child grows in experience and skill, you can put out more complicated puzzles. You will detect feelings of real accomplishment as the child meets each new challenge successfully.

Blocks.   Basic blocks are used primarily for building or reconstructing the world as the child sees it, for balancing, and for playing out ideas. The activities are unlimited: An activity may involve placing blocks one along side another to form a road or track, piling them up, or putting many of them together to form a platform on which to stand.

ABC blocks are blocks that have the alphabet letters printed on them. A child may select a certain block because of the symbol it displays. The letters may be identified or matched, as the child builds a wall, balancing tower, or some other creation.

Refer to concepts developed through block-building in other sections, such as "Reading Readiness," "Science," and "Mathematics."

Beads.   A child may string beads of different shapes and colors on a shoelace or a string. This requires selection on the child's part, as well as sufficient coordination to put the end of the lace through an opening. One bead at a time is added until the lace is full or the child is satisfied.

Small Plastic Bricks.   Realistic shapes, such as houses, towers, bridges, and free-form objects can be constructed by fitting the bricks together.

Hammer and Nails.   After a child has had some experience with a hammer or mallet and has learned to strike large objects squarely, using a hammer-nail set is a good next step in coordination development. Small, colored, geometric wooden shapes are nailed to a soft board. Each shape has a hole in the center through in the nail is placed. The child may put the shapes into a design or nail them at random to any part of the board surface. (See "Carpentry for Children" in this section.)

Parquetry Set.   Geometric shapes in assorted colors are put together inside a frame to form different designs. This involves matching colors and shapes. Children may want to sort and arrange matching colors or matching shapes, or they may enjoy piling similar shapes one on top of the other.

Dressing Frames.   Five individual frames offer learning experiences in zipping, tying, buttoning, hooking, and snapping clothes.

Counting Frames.   Ten rods with 10 matching balls mounted on each rod make up each frame. The child counts as he moves the beads from side to side.

Stacking Discs.   Perforated discs of graduated sizes and various colors are placed on a vertical rod.

Barrels.   Six barrels of graduated sizes and different colors fit one inside another. The child separates each nested set and then reassembles it in proper order.

Clock.   Movable hands help the child to become familiar with their various positions.

Dominoes.   A variety of experiences in matching are provided by four sets of dominoes featuring either numbers, colors, shapes, or animals. At first the child may simply build "trains" by placing matching pieces end to end. As he becomes more knowledgeable, he develops simple games.

Sequence Boards.   Five pieces, notched for proper sequence, tell a nursery-rhyme story when they are correctly joined.

Spinner-board Games.   Board games designed to give experience with colors and shapes are useful with the young child in the home. A player spins a pointer to a color or shape which indicates which piece he should move on the board.

Lotto Boards.   Simple variations of this old game stress color, shapes, familiar objects, and numbers.

Lincoln Logs.   This wooden building set supplies construction pieces: wooden girders with precut holes, roofs, and chimneys.

Carpentry for Children.   Carpentry is a visual experience, a motor experience, and a problem-solving experience. Construction of small and useful objects with scraps of wood, tools, glue, and various accessories helps the child gain knowledge of tools and their uses and develop a better idea of how familiar objects are made. This kind of awareness may encourage children to have more respect for materials and furniture and a greater appreciation of the roles of different workers in the community.

Woodworking develops the ability to plan several steps in sequence, in working toward a finished product. Woodworking develops inventiveness, too. Wood can be combined in all sorts of ways with other materials to achieve useful products as well as real art forms. Because most of the materials are scrap, it can be a very inexpensive activity. Woodworking also helps a child visualize a three-dimensional outcome and learn specific physical skills in using tools.

When a child is involved in carpentry, he develops in a very meaningful way the ability to visualize and select wood and accessories; to work with all kinds of tools (hammer, saw, screwdriver, plane, chisel, jigsaw, vise, drill, clamp, file); to perform procedures, such as sandpapering, filing, drilling, gluing, clamping, planing, drawing a plan, and measuring.

The child should be given tools that are slightly scaled down in size but are of real tool quality and proportion. There is nothing more frustrating than trying to do a real piece of work with a tool that is only a toy.

There are several varieties of nails. You should obtain the common wire ones with flat heads, as these are the easiest for children to work with. The child needs practice until his skill develops. It is a good idea to have a section of an old tree stump, a piece of railroad tie, or a very thick and firmly attached board for times when the child just wants to hammer but does not really care about the finished product.

To give the child endless possibilities for creative construction and for physical and mental development, obtain assorted sizes of screws; hooks and eyes; cup hooks; all kinds of fastening devices; wire of varying lengths and thicknesses; string; sturdy wooden rules and a long steel measuring tape; pencils; Elmer's Glue and quick-drying model-airplane cement; fabric scraps; all kinds of "beautiful junk," such as bottle caps, molded cardboard, Styrofoam, tile, and plastic objects; real paint; varnish; and a supply of brushes.

OUTDOOR PLAYGROUND EQUIPMENT

Permanent, Immobile Equipment

- Sandbox
- Swings (swing set with Jungle gym)
- Low slide
- Playhouse
- Ramp

Mobile Equipment

- Tricycle
- Pedal car
- Wagon
- Wheelbarrow
- Small cars and trucks
- Buckets
- Shovel
- Sand dishes
- Boards and boxes of varying sizes
- Sawhorse
- Broom
- Balls
- Snow shovels
- Sleds
- Wading pool
- Punching bag
- Inner tubes

Space

The child needs space in which to develop motor skills and muscular coordination, so important at this age. There should be a balance of space in the sun and shade, a hard-surfaced area should be available for using wheel toys and bouncing balls. A grassy plot for playing, running, and romping and a spot for gardening and digging add much to the play area. Manipulative skills are developed through sand play and water play, so a space for a sandbox and a space for water play are important.

Things to Look At

Bird-watching. Getting the child interested in birds makes every outing more exciting for you and the child. A bird feeder is a good way to attract birds to your yard. Even a three-year-old can easily learn to recognize the most common and striking varieties of birds: blue jays, robins, and sparrows. And he gets an enormous kick out of identifying a bird that he knows. A fine way to introduce birds is with the aid of an inexpensive bird book with good colored pictures of the most common birds of your area.

Let the child point out birds to you. Then you can sharpen his power of observation by asking questions: "What color is the bird's beak?" "How many feet does it have?" "What do the wings do when it flies?" Anything you can tell the child about the nature and habits of the particular bird you are watching will add to his interest: Mention, for example, that robins' eggs are blue and baby cardinals are brownish when they are born and do not turn bright red until they are almost grown up.

Trees and Flowers.   A small paperbound book with clear colored pictures of the most common wild flowers and a book of common trees stimulate a child's interest, and he enjoys comparing the real thing with the pictures in the book. Daisies, dandelions, violets, daffodils, tulips, forsythia—you will be amazed at how quickly and easily young children learn to identify these flowers.

Trees are less obviously differentiated, and it is likely that the young child is not aware that one tree is different from another. It is up to the adult to point out differences in bark, size, shape and structure of the leaves, and angles of the branches. You might start with the most obviously different groups of trees—evergreens and decidous trees—and let the child classify the trees as he sees them. Let the child gather the leaves and show them to you. Pressing leaves between sheets of newspaper under a heavy pile of books is also fun.

Identifying and classifying are not the only activities you can carry on with young children in regard to plants and trees. You can help the child understand some of the basic structures of plant life. The nature and function of roots can be fascinating to the child when a plant is uprooted and the child is shown how the plant takes up water. (See "Plants" for more activities.)

Other Things to Look At. If you look about with curiosity as you move around outdoors with the young child, the child will follow your example. Look under rocks and logs to see what is there. Notice the different kinds of soils, rocks, and rock formations. You do not have to keep up a steady lecture to the child; sometimes it is best to be talking to yourself about what you have found.

Young children like to collect seedpods, berries, twigs, pebbles, leaves — practically anything. This is not the sort of systematic collecting an older child may do, and a young child often loses interest in the collection soon. But the very act of picking things up and putting them into his own bag is very satisfying for him. Moveover, he is much more observant if he has a bag for collecting. Some children enjoy sorting out their collections later. A heavy-paper egg carton is a perfect sorting tray for small items, and muffin tins work well for medium-sized items. Large cans can be used to sort larger items. The collections can be also used for making nature collages. (See "Art.")

A child enjoys finding a good walking stick when he goes for a walk. For him, a stick is to drag, to poke into holes, to drop and pick up, to ride like a horse, and to fish for whales with in an imaginary sea.

If your walks are limited to pretty much the same route each time and you feel that the child's interest in the things around him is lagging, you can initiate a make-believe game. The child will probably insist on playing it from then on, elaborating on it on his own many times afterward. "Let's pretend we're really walking in a jungle," you suggest, and from there on the possibilities of the game are endless: "It's hot in the jungle, so everybody needs a fan made out of a large leaf." (A piece of paper or a hand will do.) "There are animals lurking behind the trees — lions, zebras, and elephants. There are monkeys chattering in the treetops." Four-year-olds are able to supply many of the details themselves.

Other possibilities include a trip to the North Pole, a caravan of camels crossing the desert, or a mountain-climbing expedition, ending with a ceremonious planting of a flag on the summit. While you are playing, the child is getting an excellent elementary geography lesson.

Special Outdoor Activities.   Many art activities, especially finger painting and easel painting, are more enjoyable outdoors, because the child can be messier than he is indoors. Music and dancing can be freer and more spontaneous outside, too, and these can be combined with water play and sand play, which are excellent outside activities. (See "Sand Play" and "Water Play.")

Playing ball may have to be limited to passing and rolling games since the coordination of the preschool child makes it difficult for the child to catch and throw a ball well. A child loves to hit balls with a light bat or sturdy stick as if he were playing golf. The child may also crawl on the ground and push the ball around with his head or nose.

Exercises that are so tedious for grownups are enjoyed by children when they can do them with others. Stretching way up high, touching toes, jumping and clapping, lying on the back and sitting up to touch the toes, and doing push-ups are all good. Another form of exercise is related to dramatic play: The child jumps like a kangaroo, flies like an airplane, turns like a windmill, and sways a trunk like an elephant.

Follow-the-leader is fun for the preschool child, but the most fun is being the leader and being first. Blowing soap bubbles is fun outdoors. The child enjoys catching and popping the bubbles.

SIMPLE GAMES FOR INDIVIDUALS[7]

A child can be lead into a wide variety of creative activities through the stimulus of simple rhymes whether they be sung or recited. In most of the activities, the child should be free to explore

[7]Clare Cherry, *Creative Movement for the Developing Child: A Nursery School Handbook for Non-Musicians,* rev. ed. (Palo Alto, California: Fearon Publishers, 1971) pp. 18–60.

and originate his own way of moving to the suggestions make by the verse. However, direct imitation can offer a different type of experience.

Resting Games

Little Birds

All the little birds
All asleep in their nest;
All the little birds
Are taking a rest.
They do not even twitter;
They do not even tweet.
Everything is quiet
All up and down the street.

Then came the mother bird
And tapped them on the head.
They opened up one little eye,
And this is what was said:
"Come, little birdies; it's time to learn to fly.
Come, little birdies; fly way up to the sky."

Fly, fly, oh, fly away, fly, fly, fly.
Fly, fly, oh, fly away, fly away so high.
Fly, fly, oh, fly away, birds can fly the best.
Fly, fly, oh, fly away—now fly back to your nest.

Repeat as many times as needed, allowing the child to supply appropriate actions. Use only the first part for resting.

Flower Seeds

All the little flower seeds sleep in the ground,
Warm and snuggly and tucked in all around,
Sleeping, oh, so soundly the long winter through.
There really wasn't very much else for them to do.
There really wasn't very much else for them to do.

(Repeat above 5 lines.)

Now their eyes they opened and they peeked all around.
And started to grow right up through the ground.

They grew so very slowly, but they grew straight and tall.
And their leaves they unfolded and waved at us all.
And their leaves they unfolded and waved at us all.

Then the sun shined down and made the flowers smile.
And they swayed and swayed in the breeze for awhile.
Until a big wind came and blew them all away.
And there were no more flowers that day.
And there were no more flowers that day.

Blow, blow, blow away, flowers. Blow, blow away.

Octopus

There's a big black octopus a-sleeping in the sea;
Shhhhhhhhhhhhhh! The octopus is sleeping.
Shhhhhhhhhhhhhh! The octopus is sleeping now. (Repeat.)

Yes, a big, black octopus is sleeping in the sea,
And when he wakes up he looks right at me.
He unwraps his arms and legs and starts out to swim,
And I turned right around and swam away from him.
There's a big, black octopus swimming in the sea;
He finally gets tired of trying to catch me.
He has so many arms and legs floating in the deep,
He wraps them all around himself and goes to sleep.

Crawling Games

Worms Are Crawling

Worms are crawling, crawling, crawling.
Worms are crawling, crawling all around.
    Or:
Making tunnels in and out of the ground.

Wiggly, wiggly worms are squirming all around.
Wiggly, squiggly, swiggly worms
Crawl in and out of the ground.

(This can be sung to "The Farmer in the Dell" tune.)

Bobby Snake

Oh, Bobby Snake is crawling, crawling, crawling.
Oh, Bobby Snake is crawling, crawling right to meeeee.
(Substitute the name of the child for meeeee.)
Wiggly, wiggly, wiggly snake
Is crawling, crawling all around.
Slithery, slippery, flippery snake
Is crawling, crawling on the ground.

Creeping Games

Tug boat

Come little boat, come out to sea.
Chug-chug, chug-chug, follow me.
Pull the big boat to the harbor or bay,
And tell the other boats to get out of your way.
Chug-chug, chug-chug-chug-a-tug-tug,
And tell the other boats to get out of your way.

TUNE: "Twinkle, Twinkle, Little Star"

Turtle

Tur-tle, tur-tle where are you?
Oh, you are so slow, slow, slow.
First one hand and then the other,
That's what makes you go, go, go.
Hide your winky little head,
And you cannot see, see, see.
Tur-tle, tur-tle, peek-a-boo!
Peek-a-boo at me, me, me.

TUNE: "Twinkle, Twinkle, Little Star"

Snails

(This is the same as turtle song, but
change "turtle" to "snail."

Change lines 3 and 4 as follows:
You have no hands and you have no feet;
I wonder what makes you go, go, go.)

Walking and Running Games

Baby

Now the little baby is learning how to walk,
Little, tiny baby that cannot even talk.
See the little baby, see how he walks so slow.
Walking little baby, now show us how you go. "Maa-maa."

Now the little baby is learning how to run,
Little tiny baby that wants to have some fun.
(Repeat lines 3 and 4.)

Little Man-Big Man

The little, tiny man
Takes little, tiny steps.
Oh, the little, tiny man
Takes little, tiny steps,
 little, tiny steps,
 little, tiny steps.
The little, tiny man
Takes little, tiny steps.

VARIATIONS: Funny crooked man takes funny, crooked steps.
     Big, fat man takes big, fat steps.
     Great, big man with big, giant steps.

SIMPLE GAMES FOR GROUPS[8]

Color Tag

Assign each child a color (or animal name, or other distinguishing name). Choose one child to be it. It stands by the adult or at an-

[8]June Chapman, *"Action Games for Little Folks"* collection of unpublished games, mimeographed.

other designated spot. It calls, "Blue!" or another assigned name. "Blue" runs to a point, such as a tree, and back to his place. It chases blue and tries to catch him. When it catches blue, the captured child becomes it, and "it" chooses a friend to take the next turn.

High Jump

EQUIPMENT: Jumping rope

Two children (or adults) hold the rope by the ends. All other children jump over the rope. Each time around, the rope is raised.

When it is so high a child cannot make the jump, he is out or is allowed to hold the rope end. Continue until only one or two winners are left.

VARIATION: The adults hold the rope and the child jumping tells the adults if he wants them to raise or lower the rope.

Obstacle Course

EQUIPMENT: Tables and chairs, boxes, boards, and the like.

Make an obstacle course of tables, chairs, or anything else you can find. Direct children to go under, over, around, through, on top of, or between obstacles.

The children learn to follow directions and learn the terms used in the game.

Pass

EQUIPMENT: Bean bags (ball or other items)
            Music or whistle

The children stand in a circle on the floor. They pass the bean bag until the music stops or until the whistle blows.

Whoever is caught with the bag goes to the center of the circle or outside the circle.

Guess Who

EQUIPMENT: Blindfold

Seat the children in a circle. After one child is blindfolded, the seated children change places. The blindfolded child then sits on the lap of a child and asks him to grunt like a pig, moo like a cow, or make a noise like some other animal. The blindfolded child guesses whose lap he is sitting in.

VARIATION: The blindfolded child sits on a chair in the center of the circle and points to someone who must make a noise like an animal.

Bunny Rabbit

Make a circle of children, who hold hands. Now tell them to spread out as wide as they can and drop hands. Choose a child to be it. It walks around the outside of the circle touching each child and saying, "Bunny." One time he says "Rabbit" instead of "Bunny," and the Rabbit hops on two feet after it. They both hop as fast as they can and try to get back to the empty space. The rabbit is now it, and he repeats the procedure.

VARIATION: Use other animals and tell the children to run instead of hop, which may be too hard for most three-year-old children.

Fish

EQUIPMENT: Colored paper fish
A paper clip for each fish
A magnet tied to a pointer

Children are seated on the floor at the outside of a large rug or in a circle. The center becomes the pond, where the paper-clipped paper fish are swimming. Each child has a turn to go fishing. When a fish is caught, the child names the color of the fish he has caught.

VARIATION: Children may also fish for numbers or letters.

Statues

One child swings each of the others. As he lets go, the child who has been swung freezes in the position in which he lands.

Guesses as to what the statue looks like.

Hot and Cold

EQUIPMENT: Any item that can be hidden

When one child leaves the room, a child is chosen to hide an item such as a block. The child returns and tries to find the hidden object by moving about in the room. If he goes away from the hidden item, the children say, "Cold." If he goes in the direction of the item, they say, "Warm." When he gets quite near, they say, "Hot." When he has found the item, he gives it to a friend to hide while another child is out of the room. (Young children require the item in plain sight.)

VARIATION: The children can sing "Bulla-bulla" or some other tune. The nearer the child gets to the object, the louder the singing, and the further away, the softer the singing.

Skipping

EQUIPMENT: Music (piano, record, drum, clapping)

All the children skip to appropriate music. When the music stops, the children freeze. The last one to stop sits down. Continue until one, two, or three children are left standing.

VARIATION: Ask the children to hop on one or both feet or run or walk, instead of skipping.

Early Bird

EQUIPMENT: Button and piece of string

The children sit in a circle, with one child who is the bird standing in the center. All the seated players grasp with both hands the piece of string, which passes completely around the circle and is tied together at the ends. A small button, the worm, has been strung on the string so that it slides easily. The bird closes his eyes, and the children pass the worm until you say, "Early Bird, open your eyes." As you say this, one child puts his hand over the button, and the bird opens his eyes.

The bird tries to guess where the worm is; the bird may have three guesses. If the bird finds the worm, he gets another turn. If he does not find the worm, he sits down and the person with the worm gets to be the bird.

Number Bounce Ball

EQUIPMENT: Ball, number cards, and music

All the children are seated in a circle. A number flasher is chosen. Music is played, and the ball is passed around the circle. When the music stops, the child with the ball stands up. The number flasher shows the child a number. The child with the ball must bounce the ball the number of time the card shows. If he does this right, he gets to be the number flasher. If he does not bounce it the right number of times, he must sit down and the game continues with the same number flasher.

Beans and Straw Relay

EQUIPMENT: Beans, jars, a straw for each child

Children are divided into two or more lines. A child at the head of the line picks up a bean by sucking in on his straw. He carries the bean on the straw and deposits it in a jar several feet away. Children in each line try to get the most beans in a jar in a given period of time.

Listen! Listen!

EQUIPMENT: Gourd or shaker

The children sit in a circle with their hands behind them. One child sits in the middle with his eyes closed. Someone is given the gourd, shakes it, and hides it behind his back. The child in the center listens. When he thinks he knows where the sound is coming from, he opens his eyes, and tries to guess which person has the gourd. If he is right, he gets another turn (limit is two turns). If he is wrong, the person with the gourd goes to the middle and the game begins again.

Policeman and the Lost Child

The children sit in a circle formation. One child is chosen to be the policeman. You pretend to be a mother who has lost a child and describe what the child is wearing. From the description, the policeman must identify the child and bring him to you. The child just described is the next policeman, and the game continues.

Who Is Gone?

The children sit on chairs in a circle. One child is chosen to sit in the middle with his eyes shut. Another child is chosen to hide in the room or go out of the room. When he is hidden, the child in the middle must figure out who is gone. Three guesses are allowed. If the guesser guesses right, he stays in the middle. If he is wrong, the person who hid goes to the middle.

Skip on Numbers

The children stand in a circle. Four numbers are drawn on the floor inside the circle. (Numbers can be taped on the floor.) Five children are chosen to skip inside the circle. Music is played. When it stops, each of the five children tries to stand on a number and call out what the number is. The child left without a number chooses someone else from the circle to take his place, and the game continues.

What Time Is It, Mr. Fox?

Mr. Fox stands about 25 feet from the group, which is in a line with you. The children ask, "What time is it, Mr. Fox?" He replies, "One o'clock." The children keep asking, and every time Mr. Fox answers, they move closer to him. Finally, Mr. Fox replies, "Dinner time!" and the children scamper back to the safe line, where they stood when the game began. Mr. Fox tries to touch all he can for his dinner.

8
social studies

Through my coming to an understanding of others' thoughts my own become clearer.

Albert Schweitzer

he social studies are those studies that provide an understanding of the physical environment and its effect upon
man's way of living, and of the basic needs of man and the
activities in which he engages to meet his needs and perpetuate
his way of life. Social studies are an important part of a child's
education, in that they help the child to understand the complex
world in which he lives and enables him to be productive and
happy within society's framework.

Education for facing such social problems cannot be delayed
until the child is older. The early years are very important, and
instruction must begin then. By means of their content, the social
studies are designed to develop intelligent, responsible, self-directing
individuals who can function as members of groups—family,
community, and world—with which they become identified. The
social studies of the preschool child must focus on the experiences
of the child in his immediate environment and the moral-social
values that his parents deem to be important.

How should a parent plan and teach in order to achieve the
desired results in the areas of environmental understandings and
moral-social values? A parent aware of the major areas of the social
studies and concepts appropriate for preschool children can find
many opportunities for helping the child to develop desirable
habits, attitudes, and skills and to gain useful information. Suggested activities in the following five areas may be helpful:

social studies activities

EVERYDAY EXPERIENCES

- Introduce new children in the neighborhood to your child. Later
talk about how children are alike and yet different. Use books,
songs, pictures, and discussion to reinforce and clarify the child's
understanding of other children and other people in the neighborhood.

- Learn about the work that fathers do. Use stories, pictures, trips, and discussion. A trip to see the child's daddy at work can do much to help the child understand and appreciate his father. Afterward help the child make a "Daddy's Work Book," by tearing out magazine pictures and pasting them on pieces of cardboard or by binding the child's drawings into a scrapbook with shoelaces. Start the book with breakfast time, and follow daddy through the day. On each page write down the child's comments about each picture, based on the child's own personal observations.

- Learn about homes in which people live: trailers, apartments, one-story houses, and larger houses. Use pictures, artwork, trips, stories, and discussion.

- Celebrate holidays by emphasizing historic significance. Use stories, trips, role-playing, music, and display objects.

- Learn how time is measured. Use clocks and calendars.

- Discuss important events in lives of people, especially the child's life. Look through photo albums, discussing the events pictured.

- Observe changes in the neighborhood or town. Discuss reasons for change.

- Learn about the ways people travel. Take a bus or train ride. Visit airports. Send messages by telephone or mail.

- Learn games and songs of children in other lands. Compare them with the child's own games and songs. Invite persons from other lands to come into your home to talk with the child. Discuss how they celebrate special holidays in their native countries.

- Talk about how different families celebrate birthdays and other holidays.

- Role-play social skills. Help the child to make choices and examine alternatives.

- Help the child observe the behavior of various groups of people — crowds, people standing together talking, and so forth.

- Arrange for puppet plays illustrating various social problems or situations that the child seems to have difficulty solving.

- Show problem-situation pictures to the child, and let him make up stories about what is happening and possible solutions.

- Encourage the child to observe other children, especially at the playground. Discuss what the child has observed.

COOPERATIVE PLANNING

Give the child opportunities to plan some of his activities. Begin with a choice between two acceptable alternatives. Later the child can organize more of his daily activities.

Let the child help plan a special event, party, trip, or excursion.

Be aware of the many opportunities to include the child in the planning of his experience.

EXCURSIONS (See also "Reading Readiness.")

Before the Trip

A trip taken without preparation is rarely as successful or meaningful to the child as a well-planned one. Discuss with the child where you are going and what you are going to see. Sometimes you can even tell the child to be alert for specific things. Use appropriate pictures, books, stories, poems, or songs to prepare the child.

Trips in the Neighborhood

Supermarket.   As eager as young children are, they have a limited attention span, so do not try to do too much. Make several trips to the supermarket, each with a different focus. Watch the goods being delivered. Watch the boxes being unpacked and merchandise stamped. Look at all the different kinds of machines in the store.

Produce Department.   What are some things displayed on special cardboard or wrapped in individual papers? Why are some things displayed on crushed ice or refrigerated? See if you and the child can name the fruits and vegetables.

161

Dairy Department.   What kinds of things are sold here? Why are they kept cold? Where do the various products come from?

Meat Department.   Watch the butcher cut and package meat. Why is the meat kept cold? Is it cold in the back, too? See how many varieties of meat you can name.

Bakery Department.   Compare the ovens with the ovens at home and the size of the flour sacks with the sacks that you buy. Notice the quantities of baked goods and the process of baking. What kinds of clothes do the bakers wear? Why?

Shoe Repair Shop.   Watch the repairman make repairs. Try to give him something that needs fixing. What kinds of machines does he have? What kinds of materials does he use? Try to get some scraps to take back for a collage.

Dry-Cleaning Shop.   What kinds of smells are in the air there? What kind of machine does he use for ironing? How does the cleaner know which clothes are yours?

Pet Store.   What kinds of pets does this store have? Are there any unusual ones? What do the various pets eat? What kinds of houses do they provide for the various pets?

Florist's Shop.   Visiting this shop is an especially good activity on a cold winter's day when everything outside is barren and bleak. A walk through the greenhouse may bring many questions to mind: Why are the flowers growing inside the greenhouse and not outdoors? What kinds of plants are there? What kinds of smells are there? How does the florist keep cut flowers from dying? Buy a plant and learn how to take care of it. The workroom, where bouquets, baskets of flowers, and corsages are assembled, will be of interest to the child.

Garage.   Watch the gas being pumped into your car's tank. Watch the gas pump itself. What is happening? Why did the bell ring? Try to see a car being raised with a hydraulic lift or a tire changed. Take the child with you when you have the oil and tires of your car checked. What kind of clothes do mechanics wear?

The Policeman and Crossing Guard.   Within walking distance of your house there is probably an intersection or a school where a policeman or crossing guard is on duty. Watch what he does. How does he tell the vehicles and pedestrians to go? To stop? The child enjoys talking to him and getting a good look at his uniform. The police station is of interest to the child, too; perhaps the desk sergeant on duty will spend a few minutes visiting with the child. He may show the child the inside of a police car, demonstrate the two-way radio, and give the child a short safety speech.

Mailman.   Make arrangements to meet your own mailman at your mailbox and then at the nearest pick-up box on the corner to watch him gather the mail. Buy a stamp and mail a letter at the post office. Children are generally not allowed in the back of most post offices, but they can see a good deal if they look through the window of the parcel-post counter. Watch the packages being weighed and mailed.

Bus Driver (Conductor).   Sit near the driver of the bus. Watch what he does. Look at his uniform.

Fire Station.   Some fire departments have open-house days. If yours does not, make an appointment for a visit ahead of time. Do not insist that the child get on the equipment, even if he is invited to do so. Climbing on an engine can be a frightening experience for some preschoolers. Usually the child is invited to try on a fireman's hat, watch a fireman slide down the pole, and inspect the engine thoroughly. Find out how the fire alarm works, where the different firemen stand on the truck, and what each of them does at a fire. Later look at fire hydrants and fire escapes in buildings. Point out fire doors and fire extinguishers or sprinklers in various buildings.

Library.   Take the child to the children's section of the library. Let him browse. Show him that all the books have letters or letters and numbers written on the bindings. Why? Perhaps your library has a storybook hour that you can attend. How does the librarian know which book you take out? Take out some books so the child can see the procedure.

Sanitation Man.   Be aware of the garbage men, street sweepers, or snowplow drivers in action and how they are dressed. Why do they wear gloves?

Demolition Site.   Why is this building being knocked down? How? What will go up here on the vacant lot?

Construction Site.   What kind of building is going up? What are the girders for? What kind of machines can you see? What do they do? How do the men dress? Why?

Repair Sites.   Observe surface or underground repair sites. What is being fixed? What equipment is in use? How are the men dressed? Why? What is under the street or sidewalk? Where did the rocks and soil come from? Try to explain to the child that the site of the city was once countryside.

Food-Processing Plant.   Any such plant is of interest to the child, whether it produces ice cream or soup. In large plants there are often guided tours and samples to taste. Call the company and ask.

Printing Plant or Newspaper Plant.   Call ahead of time and find out if tours are available and when the presses are operating. Remember to bring some paper remnants home for artwork.

Trips Outside the Neighborhood

Museum. Many communities have both science and art museums, and some have museums of natural history that are of great interest to the child. In addition, some have special exhibits for young children. Do not try to see everything at once when you take a preschool child. Go back often and take plenty of time to look and ask questions each time you go.

Farms. For the city child, farm animals are as exotic as wild ones. A farm is very exciting to the child, especially if there are some animals he can pet, feed, or hold. Be sure to watch the cows being milked and the pigs fed. Collect eggs in the hen coop, if possible, and notice the machinery, for example, tractors.

Zoos. You may know of compact zoos especially geared to young children. Such a zoo can be seen in one visit, but a larger zoo can be overstimulating if you try to see too much. Let the child know that there will be other visits to the zoo. Each time you visit, select special kinds of animals to observe, such as those with differently shaped feet and those with different tails. Find out how the animals use their feet and tails, what they do, what they eat, and how they sit and sleep.

Airports. Watch airplanes taking off and landing. How do people get on and off a plane? How does a plane get its fuel? How does a plane appear to change in size as it goes farther away? How does a plane seem to change in size as it comes closer? Why is the sound it makes louder or softer?

After the Trip

Your trip is not over just because you have returned home. You will be seeing information learned on trips displayed during block-building, dramatic play, and art sessions. But you need not wait for the child to initiate the use of this information. There are many things that you can do to help the child utilize what he has seen.

> *Discussion.*   Engage in a free discussion with the child about what he has seen. What did he see that he liked? What did he like about it? If the child brings back some small souvenir, it helps him remember. A register tape, a bag that contained animal food, a picture postcard from a museum are examples of token mementos.
>
> *Dictated Story.*   Write a story together about the trip you have taken.
>
> *Dramatic Play.*   Let the child act out the trip. (It may be the story he dictated to you.)
>
> *Art.*   You may suggest to the child that he draw or paint something about the trip.
>
> *Thank-you Letters.*   Together with the child, you might write a letter — include a picture that the child has drawn — thanking the people who helped you during your visit.

Resource People

Children learn much from a one-to-one association with adults or other children who can tell the child of their experiences. In selecting such persons, be sure that the resource person can talk with the child in a manner he can understand.

ASSUMING RESPONSIBILITY

- Help the child gain self-confidence and build a good self-image by praising him as he shows progress in assuming responsibility for his behavior and abiding by the decisions that are made.
- Discuss with the child what a family is and the responsibilities of various family members. Include not only the child's immediate family but also the extended family of aunts, uncles, cousins, and grandparents.

- Be sure the child has opportunities to come into contact with people who have different physical characteristics, different abilities, and different likes and dislikes. Discuss these with the child.

- Help the child learn to take care of his own possessions, by asking him to hang up coats where they belong and clean up after an activity. These actions help him to learn respect for personal and public property.

- Invite other children into the home so that the child has opportunities to share materials, toys, and turns at play. Other social skills that should be developed in connection with such experiences are courtesy, self-control, and interest in group activities.

- Help the child to use materials freely but without waste.

- Discuss how you cross the street and why you walk on the sidewalk. Help the child accept the limits set by the community. Discuss how rules can help us live happily together.

OTHERS' LIFE-STYLES AND CULTURES

- Cook foods from different countries. Talk about how children in various parts of the world eat and enjoy different foods.

- Use picture books that show children of ethnic minorities.

- Talk about different ethnic groups in a positive way. You should answer the child's questions directly about ethnic identity.

9
science

Never tell a child anything he can discover for himself.

Johann Pestalozzi

the young child's natural curiosity leads him to investigate and examine each new thing he finds. The beginning years of a child's life are involved in touching, tasting, smelling, looking, and listening. The child is searching for and needs to find facts and relationships that enable him to interpret and control the world around him.

By the time a child reaches school, he may have lost much of the curiosity about the world around him, and this curiosity—asking why? how? who? where? when?—is the basic outlook of the scientist. The reason for this loss of curiosity is often that the more a child can learn in a secondhand way—through words, as his language and understanding improve—the less he is encouraged to learn directly. The science part of your home curriculum should help the child keep and develop this basic curiosity. If the child is encouraged to experience life through firsthand, direct experiences and if he is encouraged to look at things questioningly, he will learn from everything around him.

The following are some specific values to be found in the science curriculum for the young child:

- He gains necessary first-hand experiences.
- He comes to know some generalizations or big meanings of science principles that he can use in solving problems in his environment.
- He increases his skill in scientific thinking.

  —Helping a child observe. One of the ways in which you guide the observations of a child is by supplying him with the correct or descriptive word as he actually makes an observation. A child who has been encouraged to observe the world in which he moves is equipped to make surprisingly good observations.
  —Helping the child see relationships. You should make a point of helping a child to enlarge each of his observations. In helping a preschool child see relationships, it is important to point out gross relationships rather than subtle ones.
  —Helping a child interpret his findings. You can suggest ideas to the child that enlarge and enrich his thinking.

- He has opportunities to use tools, equipment, and familiar materials.
- He is stimulated to satisfy his curiosity and his desire for exploration and discovery, and to seek answers to his questions.
- He learns to appreciate the world in which he lives.

You must always keep in mind that children differ not only in their capacity to learn but also in their interest in a given topic. Since the child will encounter the topic again later, it is unnecessary and very undesirable to squeeze a topic dry. In science, a topic is never mastered; it is never completed. However, we can begin very early to teach the child important concepts in science and to arouse his interests so he develops a readiness for learning and expands his interests.

How do you begin to teach science concepts to a child? The best place to begin is with the child's interests. A science lesson can often be initiated through spontaneous questions raised about a new pet, water washing sand away, a visit to the zoo, a rainstorm or the like. This does not mean, however, that you cannot stimulate the child's activities and thinking by introducing topics or ideas to create interests. The child is generally aware of the changing seasons, you might take clues from the season as to areas of study. Seasonal suggestions for science experiences are given in the following pages, along with ideas for science experiences around the house, in the kitchen, in water and sand play, and in other areas of interest to the child.

Before launching your science activities, you may want to obtain part or all of the basic science equipment, which should prove to be useful for informal exploration.

Basic Equipment

- Magnets: Horseshoe magnets, bar magnets with keepers, small container of iron filings.
- Prism

- Thermometer
- Magnifying glass
- Flashlight
- Aquarium and/or fishbowl
- Plants: Bulbs and seeds for planting
- Bug house: A place to keep worms, insects, or spiders for observation. (These can be made at home.)
- Inexpensive compass
- Binoculars
- Telescope
- Periscope
- Collection of stones, shells, seed pods, cones, and the like.

SEASONAL SCIENCE EXPERIENCES

Autumn

Harvest time

Food

      Eating and life
      Storing for winter (people and animals)
      Cooking and preparing

Seeds

Changes in plants and animals
      Caring for plants for winter
      Falling leaves
      Changing colors

Animals preparing for winter
    Birds leaving
    Nests
    Changes in fur
    Caterpillars

Weather
  Cooler days
  Effect on clothing we wear
  Frost

Winter

Weather
  Cold
        Melting and freezing
        Ice, snow, sleet, fog
        Clothing necessary
Animals
        Resting and shelter-protection
        Pets that need care
        Bird feeding
Plants
        Need for warmth and light
        Freezing-resting outside
        Winter bulbs and flowers
Heat and light
        Short days and darkness
        Awareness of moon and stars
        Warmth of sun on some days
        How buildings are heated
        Drying and evaporation
Light and Color
        Bubbles
        Prisms
        Flashlights
        Lenses
Electricity
        Clinging elements of static electricity
        Used for heat and light
        Helps us with our work

Spring

Weather
- Rain, fog, hail, wind
- Lightning, thunder
- Thawing
- Warm sun
- Effect on clothing we wear

Animals
- Baby animals
- Growth
- Homes
- Feeding and care

Plants
- Planting
- Growth
- Changes in trees and plants
- Flowers and buds

Water, sand, and mud
- Evaporation
- Absorption
- Flow and forces of water
- Mixing, dissolving, combining

Smells
- Damp things
- Flowers

Machines and their uses
- Men working after the winter
- Construction (streets and buildings)
- Tree-trimming and spraying
- Tools used on lawns, gardens, fields
- Weights and balance
- Aids to moving things

Summer

Weather
> Hot sun, shade, breezes
>
> Heat, rain, thunder, hail
>
> Effects on body (light clothing, resting, need for water, perspiration)

Animals
> Providing food, water, shade
>
> Discovery of worms, insects, spiders (how they live)
>
> Growth of baby animals born in spring

Plants
> Growth
>
> Need for sun, water, some shade
>
> Development and ripening of foods
>
> Preparing fresh fruits and vegetables

Machines
> Heavy machinery
>
> Construction
>
> Concepts of levers, wheels, pulleys
>
> Continued use of sand, mud, water

science activities

SCIENCE AROUND THE HOUSE[1]

Plumbing. Children have only vague ideas about where their bath water comes from or where it goes. They are fascinated to follow pipes back from the spigot to the individual faucets and back into the wall. If you can, shut off the wall valve and show the

[1]Marie Winn and Mary Ann Porcher, *The Play Group Book* (New York: Macmillan, 1967) pp. 124–26.

child that the water is no longer coming in. A trip to the basement will probably show the route of the incoming and outgoing pipes. The child will be surprised to see how much fatter the pipes are in the basement. Let the child play with some pipes and fittings purchased for him. (You may wish to purchase some caps, unions, couplings, tees, elbows, and nipples.)

Electricity.   Children know that plugging in appliances and flipping switches makes electricity work, but few of them know that electricity comes into their house through wires. Show the child the wiring in your house. Show him the fuses or circuit breakers and shut off the electricity in one circuit or in the whole house, if it does not make it too dark and frightening. Show the child the appliances that will not work without electricity. Take the child to the basement or outside and show him the meter. Large electric cables are usually hard to see, unless you come across a new cable being laid in the ground or an old one being replaced. Show the child static electricity with the following activities:

1. Suspend two ballons approximately five inches apart. Rub them all over with wool or fur. What happens? Rub one balloon with your hands. What happens?
2. Darken the room. Charge the balloon by rubbing it all over with wool or fur. Bring a fluorescent tube or bulb end near the balloon. What happens? What can the child say about this?

Heating.   Whatever kind of heating system your house has, there is a furnace involved. Take the child to see your furnace. Hold a pinwheel or strips of cloth or paper just above the air vent of the radiator. Then hold it below the vent or the radiator. How does the air feel up above? Does it feel the same down below? How does it feel in the room when the furnace is on?

Telephone.   The telephone is so important an item in any house that no child reaches the age of three without becoming interested in it. Let the child listen to the dial tone. Dial your own number to get a busy signal. Are the two sounds the same? Begin to dial a number—the weather number, for example,—and let the child listen to that. Do you hear anything? Complete the call. Let the child listen to the ringing sound. Does it sound like the dial tone? Like the busy signal? Let him listen to the weather forecast for the day. On one of your walks, point out telephone poles and wires. It is easy to make simple telephones that work. Take two paper cups (hot cups are the best) and punch a small hole in the bottom of each. Cut a length of string and thread its ends through the two holes, from the outside of the cup inward. Knot the ends of the string so they do not slip through the holes. The child who is the speaker covers his mouth with his cup and speaks into it. The child who is listening covers one of his ears with his cup. For the telephone to work well, the string must be held taut. The principle that explains the working of the real telephone is not the same one that explains the working of this play phone. But this simple device shows the child that telephones must be connected in someway to transmit sound.

Magnets.   Magnets never fail to fascinate children. The cheap little magnets available at the dime store are all right if you also obtain at least one good one. By handling different ones, the child can find out that magnets come in different sizes, shapes, colors, and magnetic strengths.

After the child has had an opportunity to try to pick up whatever strikes his fancy, give him a number of objects to try and your strongest magnet. Give him a box to put the attractable things in and another for things that cannot be picked up. You can even mark one box "Yes" and the other box "No." Be sure that you provide other metals besides iron or steel so the child gets the idea that only certain metals can be picked up with a magnet.

To keep your magnets in good shape, make sure they are

not purposely dropped or struck. When you put them away, place a metal keeper, which comes with most magnets, or a large nail across the ends to keep the magnets from weakening.

Other concepts that can be taught about magnets:

- Magnets can attract through different substances.
- Magnets are strongest at the ends.
- A compass needle is a magnet.
- You can make more magnets from a natural magnet.
- There are artificial magnets.
- Magnets often take their names from their shapes.

SOME PRINCIPLES OF PHYSICAL SCIENCE

As these various principles come out through the everyday experiences of the child, the parent may call attention to them through questions and suggestions for observation.

Lever.   Try to open a can of paint with the fingers, then with a screwdriver used as a lever.

Fulcrum.   Let children of different sizes ride a seesaw, which has a fulcrum in the center. What happens when the fulcrum is moved?

Balance.   Call attention to how a scale works in weighing objects. Bring an old-fashioned balance scale to the child for him to experiment with. Talk about what to do to keep from losing one's balance. Try to stand on one foot.

Inclined Plane.   Try pulling straight up a heavy object—heavy for the child—suspended from a string or rope. Then slide the same object upward along an inclined board.

Wheel and Axle.   Observe these in action on wheeled toys, faucet handles, the hands of a clock, and the like.

Gears.   Use a board with geared wheels and a crank (available in a toy store). Observe gears mesh when a hand drill is used. Look at the inside of a ticking clock.

SCIENCE IN THE NEIGHBORHOOD[2]

The streets of your neighborhood offer endless possibilities for scientific observations, such as these:

- Asphalt get soft on hot days.
- All kinds of equipment are used in repairing streets.
- Various mechanisms can be found on dump trucks and garbage trucks.
- Cranes with their pulleys or a building painter on his scaffolding dependent on pulleys. The child may want to duplicate some of these actions in his block-building.
- Merchandise is delivered into the basements of stores by means of ramps, conveyor belts, or even small elevators with visible pulleys.
- The streets are full of vehicles, all of which depend on wheels and axles.

SCIENCE IN THE KITCHEN[3]

You do not have to be a scientist yourself to help young children with science. Every time you go into the kitchen to cook, you are dealing with scientific principles.

Cooking Is Learning

Cooking is meaningful work, and it gives the child a chance to try out an adult role as well as learn some scientific principles. The child can point to the finished product as something worthwhile that he has made. Some of the other learning hidden in a well-planned cooking activity are:

[2]Winn, *The Play Group Book,* p. 126.
[3]Ibid., pp. 114-18.

- Learning to follow and interpret a recipe.
- Working together as a team with another person.
- Finding words that stand for things.
- Following directions in a certain sequence.
- Getting ideas from a book.
- Learning about quantity (weights and measures).
- Seeing changing forms of ingredients when combined, heated, or cooled.

Work Out a Sequence of Steps in Your Own Mind

Plan a series of cooking projects that become gradually more complex. Encourage the child to talk about what he is doing and relate it to scientific experiences. You may wish to begin the child's cooking experiences with recipes that do not require heat. The following sequence of cooking tasks might be helpful.

Icing. Consider making a simple icing to spread on graham crackers. This is a good first activity because only a few ingredients are needed, exact quantities are not too important, the child can add things and stir, and there is no waiting time. You might plan for the child to make icing several different times. Each time he should repeat some already familiar steps and add something new and slightly more complex, such as coloring and flavoring. Be sure to use words like liquid and dissolve.

Powdered Drinks. Children love the fruit-flavored drinks that are made by dissolving flavored sugar in water. What easier way is there to introduce the concept of solutions? Do not be afraid to use words like dissolve and solution. Dissolve some orange-drink powder in water. What happens to the orange powder? Do you think we could take the orange powder out again by pouring the drink through a strainer? (Try it.) Taste some plain water. Does it have any taste? Taste the orange drink. What gives the water its taste? Smell the plain water. Does it have a smell? Smell the orange drink. What gives the water its smell? Look at the drink. What gives the water its color?

Gelatin Desserts.   By making gelatin desserts with the child you can carry the concept of solutions even further. Start with two packages of geletin, dissolving one in hot water and the other in cold. What is at the bottom of this bowl? (Point to gelatin in cold water.) Is there any gelatin at the bottom of this bowl? (Point to gelatin in hot water.) What kind of water helps things dissolve better? Then try instant and cooked puddings. Vary these by adding chocolate bits, raisins, or pieces of canned fruits.

Butter.   All you need to make butter is heavy cream at room temperature and a jar with a couple of marbles in it. Let the child take turns with you or another child shaking the cream jar up and down until the butter begins to form. This device is much like the old butter churns. But do not expect all the butterfat to turn to butter in the time a child is willing to spend shaking. You can also make butter by beating the cream with a rotary egg beater. When you have as much butter as you want, separate the butter from the remaining liquid by using a cheese cloth strainer. Rinse the butter in cold water.

Let the child taste some heavy cream you have set aside and compare it with the liquid that was poured off. Do these two things taste the same? What did we do that made the difference? If the child is not accustomed to unsalted butter, find him a little bit of commercial salted butter to compare with it; ask him what difference he notices.

Cottage Cheese.   Most little children have no idea that the refrigerator keeps food from spoiling. They know only that it keeps things cold. Ask your child what he thinks would happen to milk if it were not kept in the refrigerator.

Place some milk in a covered container in a warm (not hot) place. You will see curds separating from whey when cheese has formed. Separate them further by using a bag made of a clean linen towel gathered at the edges. Squeeze the cheese evenly after it has stopped draining by itself. Let the child compare the smell, taste, and consistency of milk that has been refrigerated with this milk that has not.

Raisins.   Refrigeration is only one technique used to retard spoilage. Raisins are examples of a food that has been preserved by drying. Put some grapes in a sunny window and cover them with cheesecloth to keep out dirt and soot. Spread the grapes out and turn them periodically until you have raisins. You can use different kinds of grapes or currants. Leave a bunch of grapes in the refrigerator so that the child can make a comparison and actually observe what the sun does to fruit.

Raw Fruit and Vegetables.   For the child, the activity is peeling, cutting, and taking out seeds. Fruits and vegetables can be tasted raw, and some can later be boiled or stewed. This activity can lead to a lot of related discussions about how different foods look when raw and when cooked and how they feel and taste as well.

Special Projects.   Make ice cream in a freezer. Make ice cubes or Popsicles of colored and flavored water, or make ice cubes from real fruit juices. A child can prepare soup, cookies, cupcakes, pancakes, candy, and many other items with supervision.

OTHER KITCHEN ACTIVITIES (See "Plants," in this Section.)

Water Play

Water is inexpensive and readily obtainable, yet it has a natural attraction for the child. And if presented in an interesting way, it can be a great teaching material. Water is easy to work with; it yields and changes shape. It does what the child wants it to; therefore, the child feels successful when he works or plays with water. It also offers relaxation for the tired and emotionally upset child. Equipment for water play:

- Measuring cups
- Funnels
- Meat baster
- Rotary egg beater
- Piece of hose
- Empty squeeze bottles
- Boats
- Objects that float and that do not float
- Food coloring
- Small watering can with a spray attachment

Developing Concepts Through Water Play

The adult should ask these two questions time and time again in order to help the child discover concepts about water: What do you think happened? Why? The child may learn many concepts from his play with water. A few of these are:

- Generally, heavy things sink and light ones float.
- Hollow things float until they fill with water.
- Water does not go up a baster unless you squeeze the bulb.
- Blowing air into a pipe full of soapy water makes bubbles.
- Certain things, like sponges, cloth, and paper, absorb water.
- Water takes the shape of its container.
- Water itself has no color.
- Using sets of measuring cups helps the child see relationships between volumes: Two pink cups (½ cup each) fill one white cup (1 cup).

Learning Principles

Remember, help the child describe what he sees and verbalize his questions. But do not force him to give answers, and do not give him too many answers. Do not feel obligated to teach him technical terms, such as evaporation or displacement. Let him find his own operational ways of describing what he sees.

When he has a question he cannot answer (and perhaps you cannot either), help him think of some way to get closer to the answer. This is really the beginning of the scientific attitude: accurate observation and description of what is happening; formulation of experiments to find out what happened, or what could happen next; and expression of what did happen in a way that someone else can understand.

Help the child see relationships by letting him find out about the relationship of air and water. Blow to make water move, demonstrate air and water pressure, and siphon water from one vessel to another. What happens when you force water through a small opening? Pour water into different substances? Try to force it to stay in a confined space?

Evaporation. Observe the difference in the rates of evaporation from a narrow-mouthed container and wide-mouthed container. Find out what the child thinks is happening to the water that disappears. Supply the word evaporation only after the child has seen and described the situation in his own words and has observed it in enough different kinds of situations to make some accurate predictions about when it happens and when it does not. Watch the evaporation of rain on the pavement when the sun comes out after a rainstorm.

Other Water Play Ideas

• Observe that water is needed to maintain life. Show what happens to a plant that is not watered.

185

- Demonstrate that water can turn solids into liquids. Dissolve sugar, salt, dry-milk crystals, or instant chocolate in water. Discuss this with the child.

- Discuss and observe sources of water: rain, faucets, reservoirs, lakes, and streams. Make rain, with a kettle of boiling water and a cold lid.

- Fill a jar half full of water and mark the waterline. Set it out doors in winter or in a refrigerator to freeze. What happens to the waterline? Melt the contents again. What happens to the waterline?

- Taste ocean water, snow, spring water, and mineral water.

- Float an ice cube on water and observe how much ice shows above the surface.

Sand Play

Sand, like water, is easy to work with. It acts like a fluid and pours, changing shape as it is poured. It offers little resistance. Sand can be played with in many ways. There is no right or wrong way to play. For this reason sand offers security to young children who are not sure about what they can do and how well they can do it. Sand can be dampened to make a different kind of material, somewhat similar to clay. There is no reason to limit sand play to the outdoor sandbox. You can set up sand play on a modified scale indoors with salt, corn meal, or flour as a substitute.[4] Equipment for sand play.

• Measuring cups	• Pails and shovels
• Funnels	• Cans and other containers
• Spoons	• Small gardening tools
• Strainers	• Sifters
• Small cars	• Gelatin molds
• Empty shakers	• Pie tins

[4]Winn, *The Play Group Book*, pp. 203-04.

- Sugar scoops
- Small plastic figures
- Watering cans
- Spatulas

Developing Concepts Through Sand Play

- Things that are bigger than the holes in a sieve do not go through.
- Things like salt and sand that are made of small (particles) pour like water and take the shape of the container they are in.
- If you wet sand, the particles stick together and you can mold the wet sand and build with it.
- If you look at sand through a magnifying glass, some of the particles are shiny.

SOUND

Learning about sounds and how they are made offers much opportunity for experimenting. Listen to many sounds, such as those made by musical instruments, trains, jet planes, and echoes, to see how different they are.

Learn that sound is made by motion or vibration by going through these exercises:

- Hit a drumhead or cardboard carton to make the surface vibrate.
- Run a bow over a violin or strum a guitar to see strings vibrate.
- Blow into tops of wide-mouthed bottles and soda-pop bottles and listen to the differences in tone. Fill the bottles with water to various levels and blow into the bottles. What happens to the sounds?
- Remove the cover of a piano and watch the wires vibrate when the keys are struck.
- Stretch elastic bands over a shoebox and pluck them. Use bands of various thicknesses. Listen for differences in the sounds.
- Feel your own throat when you talk.

AIR AND AIR PRESSURE

Help the child understand that air is all about us and acts in many ways. Demonstrate how air in motion exerts pressure.

- Blow fuzz from a dandelion.
- Watch birds flap their wings to stay up.
- Feel air coming from a tire pump.
- Walk against the wind. In what ways can you tell that the wind is moving? Does the wind seem to blow from any particular direction? How can you tell?
- Learn that air has volume (takes up space). Give the child a small, clear plastic bag and show him how to catch air in the bag. Let the child punch a hole in the air-filled bag to feel the air rush out.
- Put an empty bottle into water and see bubbles escape. Do the same with a blown-up balloon.
- Help the child understand that oxygen is necessary to life and that air contains oxygen. Discuss the hazards of plastic bags. Observe the need for air holes in insect jars or animals' boxes.

WEATHER AND SEASONS

Changing seasons of the year bring holidays and exciting activities. Children have some awareness of the natural cycles. They are interested in weather and seasons and in knowing how these affect the habits of living creatures, including themselves.

- Observe the weather each day. Encourage your child to keep a record of changes on a weather chart made from oak tag, with pictures of sun, wind, rain, clouds and snow.
- Does your child know the words to describe weather—cold, warm, sunny, cloudy, rainy, foggy, windy, or stormy? Can he tell the difference between rain, snow, sleet, fog, mist, drizzle, thunder, lightning, a blizzard, or a hurricane? These are not

words or concepts to be taught in isolated ways but things to be observed and talked about as it happens.

- Notice the kinds of clouds that occur under various weather conditions (rain, wind, sun, or heat).

- On a partly cloudy day, notice the variations in light and shade as clouds move across the sun. Can the child watch the sky and predict when there will be sunlight? Do we see shadows when it is cloudy?

- Encourage the child to try to forecast the weather by watching the sky. Listen to a weather forecast on the radio after making your own.

- Put a thermometer in the hot sun and another in the shade. Note the difference in the mercury column. Take a thermometer from a refrigerator and place it near a stove. Note the rise in temperature. Let the child try to explain the change. Use indoor and outdoor thermometers and record temperature changes for a week or a month.

- On a rainy day, put a pie pan outside to catch the rain. Measure the amount of water that falls in the pan in a certain period of time.

- Observe a puddle of water after a rain. What happens to that puddle on a hot day? On a cold day? Talk about evaporation. You might also hang a wet towel outside in the sunshine and check it several times while it dries.

- Observe the effects of temperature changes upon plants, animals, and people.

  —How do trees look at different seasons? Draw pictures of them.
  —Why do few flowers grow in winter?
  —What happens to animal fur when the weather turns cold?
  —How do people dress in the rain, snow, or sun?
  —How do birds keep warm in winter?
  —How do people act when a room is too hot? Too cold?

- Look at a rainbow. Make a rainbow with a prism or a stream of water from a hose in the sunlight.

- Watch lightning or listen to thunder. Which comes first? Why?
- Catch snowflakes on a dark paper and look through a magnifying glass.
- Discuss weather, seasons, and holidays. Can the child relate certain kinds of weather to the seasons in which they normally occur? Are there any seasonal events that do not change? Does each one of us always have a birthday? A Thanksgiving? What are some activities which will help the child to appreciate and really see the uniqueness of each season.

THE EARTH

- Make rock collections; feel the textures and weights of different kinds.
- Compare different kinds of soils in your area: sand, humus, clay, and so on.
- Take field trips to observe the terrain: hills, gullies, valleys, prairies, and rock slides.
- Display items made from earth materials: bricks, glass, ceramics, jewelry, and coins.
- Observe changes made on the earth by weather:

    — Pour water over a mound until a gully is created.
    — Watch the wind redeposit leaves and soil in different parts of the yard and cause snow drifts.

- Make sand by rubbing pieces of sandstone together.
- Visit exhibits or sites of oil production, coal- or ore-mining, brick-making, concrete-mixing, or other industries that are important to your area and makes use of materials from the earth.

THE EARTH'S NEIGHBORS

- Talk about what is in the sky.
- Learn the general directions in relation to your home: The morning sun seems to come up in the east; sunset is in the west; cold winds come from the north; and birds fly south in the winter.

- Observe that the sun shines on us by day; learn that it shines on the other side of the world when we have night. Demonstrate with a tennis ball or globe marked with the location of the city you live in. Shine a flashlight (sun) on the ball (earth) and rotate the ball so that the marker is sometimes under the sun and sometimes in the shadow.

- Discuss what the sun does for us: It makes plants grow, provides warmth and light, makes shadows, and lights the moon.

- Discuss the need to protect eyes from the glare of the sun, bodies from burning, and clothes from fading.

- Observe cloud formations in the sky and discuss why they belong to earth rather than to outer space.

- Discuss the kinds of clouds that bring rain.

- Observe shadows made by the sun at different times of day.

PLANTS

Children generally enjoy looking at and caring for plants. And those children who have frequent experiences with seeds and growing plants absorb some basic understanding of life processes.

Trees.   Trees are very useful to man and can provide some worthwhile learning experiences for the young child.

- Call trees by their specific name: pine, oak, and maple.
- Notice the sizes, shapes, and ages of different trees.
- Observe that many trees lose their leaves in the winter.
- In the spring note that the leaves come out first on some trees, and blossoms come out first on others.
- Observe the grain of wood and the rings on a cut tree.

Looking at Leaves.   The child can collect and examine many different leaves. How many different shapes can you find on one plant? On different plants? What are some good words to describe these different shapes? Are leaves all the same shade of green? Are all leaves green? Notice how the newest leaves are usually lighter in color.

- Do all leaves feel the same? What are the different textures, and how can you describe them?
- Make a guide to all the different kinds of plants in your yard by collecting a leaf from each. Leaves can usually be preserved by pressing them between two pieces of waxed paper with a warm iron.

Looking at Seeds.   The child can actually watch seeds germinate, if you put some dried beans in a small container lined with damp (not soggy) paper toweling, tissue, or cotton. You can use the caps of large detergent bottles, empty eggshells, or cut-down milk cartons as containers.

- To show the germination of another kind of seed, follow the same procedure with some corn seeds or grass seeds. A sprouting bean has two seed leaves (cotyledons), the sprouting corn or grass seed only one.
- You and your child can see the seed coat shrivel and fall off, as first the roots and then the stem begins to emerge from the seed.
- Plant some of the germinating seeds in soil. Leave some in water. Which ones eventually die?
- You can see the seed leaves shrivel and die, as the true food-making leaves develop.
- Your kitchen can supply you with many of the seeds and plants that you and your child may want to grow.

Carots, Turnips, and Other Root Vegetables.   Chop off all but an inch of the green tops. Place the root top in a shallow dish of water, root end down. The green top begins to sprout anew in a week or two, and it may blossom, although no new vegetable will grow.

Onions.   To make an onion sprout, place the onion on the rim of a jar of water, root end down and touching the water. If it is kept in a warm, dark place, it begins to sprout in a few days.

Yam, Sweet Potato, and Other Tubers.   Put one end of your tuber into a jar of water and keep it in a warm, dark place until sprouting begins. Try cutting a potato into sections — an eye to a section — and planting them in a garden.

Avocado.   The seed of an avocado or alligator pear develops into a tall plant. Place the flat end of either down in a jar of water. Only the end should touch the water, so you may want to support the seed by pushing one or more toothpicks into each of three sides, and resting the toothpicks on the lip of the jar. Once the roots begin to grow, they must be planted in soil. Pinch back the plants once they are about nine inches high, to make them lusher and less spindly.

Pineapple.   It can be grown in much the same way as a carrot, from the top inch of the fruit and the greens, cut from a whole pineapple. It is a good idea to dry this top for a few days, as the pineapple flesh may rot otherwise. This top section may then be rooted by being placed in the mouth of a jar filled with water, with the fruit portion touching the water.

Other Things to Observe about Plants

- Discuss ways in which seeds are carried: spread by wind, water, and man; sticking to the fur of animals; being eaten and excreted by animals; and carried off by squirrels and other animals.
- Watch plants bending toward the light. Conduct a controlled experiment in which some plants are turned daily and others are never turned. Also observe the differences in plant growth on a series of cloudy days and a series of bright sunny days.
- See what happens to grass when it is covered by a rock or board for several days. Discuss what plants and grass need in order to grow well. Do all need the same conditions?
- Take walks to identify local shrubs and trees; general shape, color, and foliage.
- Learn the general differences between deciduous and evergreen trees (spring blossoms and changing and falling leaves). What kinds of trees are Christmas trees?
- Visit a tree farm or forest to see trees in various stages of growth.

- Count the rings in a log or stump to learn the age of a tree.

- Feel bark, smell pitch, and listen to the sound of the wind through the branches of a tree.

- Observe how crabgrass spreads and chokes out lawn grasses.

- Look at different kinds of wild grasses in an empty lot.

- Raise molds on stale bread or an orange rine placed in a jar with damp blotters and left in a warm, dark place. Examine molds with a magnifying glass.

- Plant and care for a flower garden or visit nearby gardens. See how different types of flowers grow and observe seasonal differences in varieties of flowers.

- Make pleasing flower arrangements. Enjoy the beauty, form, color, and fragrance of garden flowers.

- Learn to identify the main parts of a flower: stem, leaves, petals, sepals, and calyx

- Discuss the parts of plants that people eat: seeds of grains, leaves of green vegetables, roots or tubers of some yellow vegetables, stems of asparagus, seed pods of green beans, sprouts of beans, root nodes of potatoes, sap of maple trees, buds of artichokes, and so forth.

ANIMALS

The animal world rates high in interest for most children. Children can learn about animals in many ways:

- During a day, see as many animals as possible. Draw a picture of each animal that you have observed and talk about what each animal was doing. Call the animal by a specific name, for example, by the breed of dog (collie, dachshund, and so on).

- Find a small animal, such as an ant, fly, or worm, and look at it through the magnifying glass. See if it has any hair on its body. See how many new things you can discover about that animal.

- Compare baby animals with their mothers. The babies are

SMALLER ANIMALS AND THEIR CARE

Animals	Feeding	Housing
Lizards	Mealworms, flies, other insects	Provide a terrarium with sand; sprinkle with water several times a week; some direct sunlight is helpful.
Guinea pigs, hamsters, rabbits, mice	Dry alfalfa pellets, grain, vegetables, meat scraps	Cage should be about four times larger than animal (apple-box size); provide sleeping box; keep clean and provide water.
Snakes	Large insects, lizards, mice. (If snake does not feed, release it)	Provide a cage as long as the snake; arrange a woodland habitat.
Salamanders, newts	Insects, earthworms	Keep in moist, woodland habitat; animals escape readily.
Tadpoles	Algae, cooked lettuce or spinach, meat scrapings	Provide an aquarium with rocks that stick out of water.
Turtles	Mealworms, earthworms, lettuce	Provide land and water habitat.
Tortoises	Lettuce, soft fruits	Provide water, but keep cage dry.
Parakeets and other birds	Parakeet seed or other bird seed, calcium or a cuttlebone	Place cage away from direct sun and drafts. Cover cage at night. Keep fresh gravel paper on bottom of cage. Add fresh water daily.

smaller and they usually are a different color. Learn the names of baby animals: cow, calf; cat, kitten; sheep, lamb; dog, puppy; horse, colt; and goat, kid.

- Pets can provide valuable learning experiences. Besides the common cat and dog varieties, consider keeping one of the following smaller animals listed in the chart: Smaller Animals and Their Care.

The child can learn about animals from stories, books, and songs.

- Arrange for the child to listen to a record about an animal. Then he might draw what he thinks the animal would look like.

- Encourage the child to make up his own stories about an animal and tell them to someone or record them on tape.

- After listening to a story about an animal, ask the child to pretend to be that animal and role-play to show what that animal did in the story.

- Learn songs and riddles about animals. There are many Mother Goose rhymes about animals that the child will enjoy learning: "Hickory Dickory Dock," "Three Blind Mice," "Hickety Pickety," "Ride a Cockhorse," "Tom," and "Hey, Diddle Diddle."

There are many places to go and see animals. Visit a farm, zoo, field, stream, and other animal homes and then carry out some of the following activities:

- Watch a cow being milked.

- Observe the kind of food which farm animals eat and find out how they get it.

- Gather eggs.

- Talk about the ways the various animals help us or what they provide for us.

- Upon returning from a visit to the farm, ask the child to select animal models or pictures of animals that are found on a farm. The child might draw some of the animals he saw.

- Make a farm animal from clay and display it.

- Make a barn and silo from boxes — the silo walls from two large, round oatmeal boxes glued together and its roof from a light-weight cardboard circle. Paint them and add blocks and rubber or wooden animals.

- Visit a zoo and tell the child the names of the different animals, or ask the child to tell you the names. Observe each animal for a while to see if you can discover what it eats, how it moves, and what sounds it makes. Compare the feet, heads, tails, and ears of various animals.

- Collect pictures of zoo animals and glue them on paper to make the child's own zoo book.

- Dig up a piece of soil from a field or wooden lot. Place it in a clear jar. Place the jar in a warm, sunny window. What do you see? Draw pictures of the animals you see.

- Take a walk with your child and examine grassland, wooded areas, freshwater ponds and streams, old stumps, and tree trunks. Look under rocks, boards, and fallen logs. Examine the foundations of buildings. Look through all kinds of debris, and examine soil around shrubbery or in the garden. Collect some of the small animals you find and place them in a terrarium or an insect cage.

- Make an aquarium so the child can observe water life at home.

- Go for a walk and watch for birds, or scatter crumbs and seeds for the birds to eat.

- Look at pictures of animals and note where the animals live: on the ground, in the ground, in trees or bushes, in the water, and on land.

- Take a walk and look for birds' nests, spiderwebs and other animals' homes. But do not disturb the homes.

Animals use different parts of their bodies to move.

- Collect pictures of animals that run very fast. Make up riddles to go with each picture.

- Make a clay model of an animal that jumps or one that hops or swims or flies.

- Look at pictures of animals that jump or hop, and discuss how their legs are similar.

- Watch an animal run. Does it run on the tips of its feet or does it run flat-footed? Let the child demonstrate.

- Look at an insect wing under the magnifying glass. Notice the color, size, shape, and veining.

- Collect some pictures of animals that fly. Study their wings to see how they are alike and how they are different.

- Study pictures of animals that climb, to see how they are alike and how they are different.

- Examine the hands or paws or legs of animals that climb. Do they have fingers? Do they have claws? What do they have to help them climb?

- Notice the fins of the fish in the aquarium, and discuss how a fish uses its fins. Which fins are used to steer the fish?

- Examine the feet of a duck, and tell how many toes it has.

- Examine the toes of a frog, and tell how they are similar to those of other animals that swim.

- Place a worm on a moist blotting paper in a shallow dish and describe its color, shape, and size. How does the worm move? Does it wiggle from side to side or move in a straight line? Pick up the worm, and feel the bristles on the lower side of its body. What are they for? Touch the worm lightly with a pencil in different places. Where is it most sensitive?

- Examine the snails in an aquarium and in a terrarium. Note the way they move on their broad muscular feet.

Animals need the energy they get from food to live and grow.

- Find pictures of animals that eat plants and put them in a booklet for future reference.

- Study the mouths of animals that eat plants. How are they similar? Notice the ways the animals who eat plants get their food.

- Collect pictures of animals that eat animals, and explain how their teeth are adapted for the purpose. Look at their mouths and feet.

Animals protect themselves in many ways.

- Discuss animals that move very fast to escape danger. Read or make up a story about an animal that runs very fast to escape danger.

- Compare the legs of fast-running animals with those of animals that hop or jump.

- Discuss and 'find some pictures of animals that hold very still so they cannot be seen easily by their enemies.
- Draw a picture of a frog on a lily pad so that it can barely be seen.
- Observe animals that use their body parts to fight their enemies.
- Discuss ways you have of protecting yourself from an enemy.

Animal babies are born in different ways.

- Discuss animal babies that are hatched from eggs.
- Collect frog eggs and watch them hatch.
- Watch for opportunities to see baby animals that are born alive.
- Compare the number of babies a mother bear has with the number a mother frog has.

We group or classify animals that are alike.

- Animals without backbones are called invertebrates. Examine a worm to see if it has a backbone. Also examine a clam, oyster, snail, crab, spider, grasshopper, or butterfly.
- Animals with backbones are called vertebrates. Some of these are fish, amphibians, reptiles, birds, and mammals. Obtain a dead fish that has not been cleaned. Instruct the child to cut it open with some help from you. Find the backbone and other bones.
- Find pictures of various vertebrates. With a red crayon, color the area where you would find the backbone. Do the same with pictures of birds, and other vertebrates.
- Instruct the child to pretend to be a mammal of some kind (dog, horse, or monkey) and show how the animal's body would be without a backbone.

Some animals are helpful to man.

- Ask the child to name some of his favorite foods and find out if any of these come from animals.

- Cut out pictures of food that animals provide for man.
- Visit a grocery store, and notice the food that is provided by animals.
- Look at what the child is wearing to see if anything comes from an animal.
- Show the child samples of materials that are provided by animals.
- After a visit to a farm, discuss ways a farmer uses animals.
- Visit a blind person who owns a Seeing-Eye dog, and ask him to tell the child about his dog.
- Discuss some animals you think would make good pets for the child and your reasons. Also talk about animals that would not be good pets and tell why.
- Arrange for the child to keep and care for a pet in the home.

OUR BODIES

Man uses his senses—touch, taste, smell, sight, and hearing—to help him learn more effectively and live better. (See also "Vocabulary Development.")

Touch

The Feel Box.   Fill a box with various objects and then ask the child to put his hand inside an opening. Ask, "Can you guess what is inside just by feeling it? Describe what you feel to a friend, and see if he can guess what it is."

- Have the child feel various objects—hard, heavy, light, soft, cold, smooth, furry, rough, and sticky—and then tell how they feel.
- Put a blindfold on the child, and see if he can identify different fruits by the way they feel.
- Use a magnifying glass to look at the following object: salt, sugar, sand, and coral. Now feel the objects. Ask "How do they look? How do they feel?"

- Make a collage with at least five materials of different textures.
- Touch different parts of skin with a feather, a piece of ice, and a pin. Ask, "Where is it more sensitive to the pin? To the ice? To the feather? What can you say about this?"

Taste

- Hold your nose and eat a soda cracker. "Does it taste the same?" (Much of what we think is taste is really smell.)
- Place salt, sugar, baking soda, and lemon juice in separate cups for the child to taste. "How were they different? What did they taste like?"
- Have the child taste various foods: powdered sugar, salt, crackers, flour, lemon, sugar, honey, baking soda, vanilla, wet mustard, and vinegar. Then ask the child to tell you if each tastes salty, bitter, dry, sour, or sweet.
- Look in a mirror, and observe the bumps on the surface of your tongue. The sensation of taste is located in clusters of cells called taste buds. They are spread unevenly over the tongue. The taste buds can recognize only four stimuli: sweet, sour, salty, and bitter. Taste buds at the tips of the tongue are sensitive to sweetness and saltiness. Along the sides, the buds are sensitive to sourness, and in the back, bitterness. Many foods have more than one taste.
- Using a medicine dropper, put different substances—water, vinegar, salt, sugar, and mixed cocoa and water—on different parts of the tongue. Rinse the mouth after each one. Which area of the tongue told you what it was? What can the child say about this experience?

Smell

- Smell various items, but do not take too big of whiffs! Examples: pepper, cinnamon, Mentholatum, sour milk, perfume, cloves, vanilla, and flowers. Tell about the smells.

- Look at pictures of things that have smells. Describe what the smells would be like if the pictures were real.
- Open a bottle of perfume or something with a strong smell. Watch how the smell spreads through the room.

Sight

- Look at two objects. Which one do you think is the larger? Smaller? Fatter? Thinner? Taller? Shorter?
- Look at various pictures. What shapes can you see in each picture? How many different shapes? How many of each shape?
- Look at a tray of three to five objects. Remove one of the objects when the child is not looking. Now ask the child to guess which object was removed.
- I-spy. Describe an object in the room by shape, color, or size. Ask the child to guess the object you are thinking about. Encourage the child to try to describe the object.
- Describe a person that you and the child know. See if the child can guess who it is.
- Identify various objects from their silhouettes.
- Draw a picture while you are blindfolded.
- Tear an object out of paper wrappings behind your back.
- Put a blindfold on and tie a shoe or button a button.
- Look at your eyes in a mirror. What can you learn about your eyes?
- Ask someone to stand in very bright light. Watch his iris and pupil. What is happening to them? Ask him now to cover his eyes for a minute or two. Then observe what happens. What can you say about this?
- Count the number of time a person blinks in a minute.
- Identify the colors in a room. How many different colors can you see? Now blow soap bubbles and list the colors you see.
- Mix colors and see what other colors you can make.
- What happens when you put a prism in a light beam? What can you say about this? Draw a picture of the rainbow and the colors you see emerging from the prism.

- Fill a jar with water, and put a ruler in the jar. What do you observe? What can you say about this?

Hearing

- Put an object in a box and see if the child can guess what it is by the way it sounds when you shake it. You may have to first show the child several objects, such as a spoon, handkerchief, wooden block, and apple, and then select from these items.
- Tape-record various sounds, such as an eggbeater, siren, children, a crying baby, shouting mother, buzzing saw, the telephone, a dog, doorbell, piano, car, and dripping water. Listen to the tape and see if the child can identify the different sounds.
- Place a few objects on a table: a metal spoon, pin, book, and the like. Drop the objects one by one when the child is not looking, and see if he can name each object dropped.
- Look at pictures: a frog, bird, and dog. See if the child can describe the sounds these pictures would make if they were real. Is the sound deep, high, soft, or what?
- Do a rhythm pattern and see if the child can repeat it. Repeat with the child producing the pattern.
- Stretch a rubber band across an object. Pluck it. What happens?
- Fill four soda-pop bottles with water to different levels. Tap the bottles with a pencil. What happens? What can you say about this?

It is important for us to eat good food every day, to give us energy, help us grow, and make us healthy.

- After playing a strenuous game, ask the child how he gets so much energy to play.
- Ask the child what happens when you go for a long period of time without food. Compare a person to a car that needs gas to go.
- All living things need water to grow. Show a growing plant that has not been watered for a long period of time. (Be sure to give the child a drink of water often.)

- Ask the child what would happen if he ate only one kind of food, like candy.
- Ask the child to name all the kinds of meat products he knows about. Show pictures of different animals, and let him decide which animals we get our meat from. Explain that there is protein in meat.
- Show pictures of other foods containing protein.
- Ask the child to find a muscle in his body. There are 650 muscles in our body, and they give us the ability to move. We need protein to be able to use our muscles.
- Prompt the child to draw his favorite fruits and vegetables. Vitamins come from fruits and vegetables. Discuss how vitamins help us in many ways.
- Try some new and unusual fruits and vegetables.
- Talk about the child's favorite cereal, and explain that it contains grain.
- Talk about other foods that contain grain.
- Visit a bakery or bake some bread at home, explaining that flour is made from grain. Grain gives us a major source of energy.

Rest and exercise are important for good health.

- Instruct the child to say the words rest and exercise. Show the child pictures of people resting and exercising, and ask the child to identify what the people are doing.
- Do various exercises with the child and then rest for 10 minutes. Discuss the fun you had exercising. Discuss how good it feels to rest afterward.
- Allow the child to mention different ways we can exercise: walking, dancing, doing stunts, bike-riding, swimming, playing, and working. Draw pictures showing some of these activities.
- Talk about ways to rest: Listening to stories or soft music, looking at a picture book, or drawing quietly.
- Let the child draw his own face when he is rested and when he is tired.

Good mental health is important.

- Our faces show how we feel. Make various facial expressions showing that you are happy, sad, frightened, or loving.

- There are many things we can do to release our feelings. Try punching a bag, molding with clay, or playing in the water to help you feel better.
- We feel differently at different times. Show pictures of people doing different things: playing, working, fighting, or jumping. Ask how each person feels. Why? How would you feel?
- We can talk about some of our feelings. When we are angry, it is all right to tell others that we are angry.
- Others are important to us. Encourage the child to name some of the people who are important to him.
- Sometimes we are really angry at those we love. Tell about some of these times.

Safety is important for a happy, healthy life.

- Talk about safe practices that are observed around the home, away from home, and on trips.
- Draw pictures of children playing safely.

10
mathematics

I know one—there's only one of me.

Barbara Hazen

the young child spends much time in searching for meanings, and it is this search that motivates him to question, to investigate, and to try and try again a given task. Finding answers to questions brings the real excitement of discovery to the child.

A parent utilizes the young child's innate search for meanings as he provides situations in the child's environment to challenge him and also to provide many and varied experiences by which he can develop mathematical concepts and skills. Meanings can best be developed by the child through his own experiences, not by rote memory.

Mathematics is a big part of a child's everyday life — going shopping for a dozen eggs or a quart of milk, dividing a cookie, putting one seed in one hole when planting, and so on. Life is full of real and meaningful mathematical experiences that a parent can utilize. However, the conceptual learning is strengthened when these experiences are extended by new, planned situations involving the same skills and yet contributing to a broader understanding.

Some general objectives for a mathematical program are:

- An understanding of mathematical ideas.
- The ability to solve problems.
- An atmosphere for creative thinking.

In a parent's eagerness to help his child achieve the above objectives in the mathematical curriculum, he must keep some basic facts in mind:

- Concepts are built up gradually.
- Ideas are developed to the point of real understanding before adding technical terminology and symbols.
- Ideas are associated with environmental situations.
- The introduction of new material is governed by the concepts that the child has already mastered.
- The instructional mathematics program is developed as an integral part of the total curriculum.

Activities for developing basic skills are included here, but a parent should utilize the everyday experiences of the child whenever possible, to teach the skills listed and to achieve the above objectives in a mathematical program.

mathematics activities

VOCABULARY

The child acquires a vocabulary of number names (numerals) and an understanding and use of quantitative words.

As a part of the child's daily routine, include the following terms and demonstrate their meanings:

big and little	same length
long and short	highest
high and low	lowest
wide and narrow	longer than
late and early	bunch
first and last	group
adding to and taking away	set
middle	pair
once	many
few	more
tall and short	most
light and heavy	twice
together	

Place emphasis upon experiences that involve mathematical vocabulary, such as grocery shopping. Tell the child you will buy a *bunch* of radishes, a *dozen* eggs, a *quart* of milk, or a *pound* of butter. Let the child hear you use the above terms often. And when the child plays store at home, there will be many opportunities to build his mathematical vocabulary.

Play a game where the child is given the opportunity to think of the largest thing he knows, the smallest, the highest, the heaviest, and so forth.

Count objects for the child so he hears the numerals often and becomes familiar with their names. Count chairs to see if there are enough for company at dinner. Count the napkins. Count the cookies to see if there are enough. Keep score when playing games. Count the bounces of a ball.

COUNTING

The child should be given many and varied opportunities to identify numerals with the number of objects.

- Counting by rote may or may not have meaning for the child. Do not mistake counting by rote as evidence of readiness to work with numbers. But begin with the child touching each object as he counts. Repeat this exercise in various experiences until this need to touch or to point to objects is no longer necessary.

- Block-building affords many opportunities to better the child's understanding of numbers. With blocks a child can visualize that the word one means / block, two means // blocks, and five means ///// blocks, and so on. The parent can ask the child to pass three round blocks, or to trade one round block for two square blocks.

- Provide for many manipulative counting situations with beads, buttons, cookies, napkins, blocks, petals on a flower, fingers, toes, chairs, steps, windows, and cracks in the sidewalk.

- Play May-I? in which a child is allowed to take a certain number of steps forward if he says, "May I?" If a child forgets to say "May I?" he must stay in his place. Use instructions, such as "Skip three times to the left." "Skip three times to the right." "Hop twice." "Take four jumps forward." "Take two hops backward."

- Identify numerals on the television screen and figures on a page, dial telephone numbers, play with number cutouts, and notice addresses on homes.

- Use rhyming words, finger plays, songs, and games that involve numbers.

- Make available large numerals that the child can manipulate, read, and place in order.

- Stretch a clothesline or string low enough so the child can see it comfortably. Using numerals printed on pieces of tagboard, pin the numerals on the line with clothespins. Pin them up in correct sequence except for one numeral, for examples, 1, 2, 4, 3, 5). The child can then correct the mistake. When the child is able, let him pin the numerals on the line.

- Write numerals on pieces of sponge or pincushions and ask the child to place the correct number of pins in each sponge or pincushion. (Make dots to indicate the number of pins if the child needs help.)

- Mark berry baskets with a numeral. Let the child place enough buttons or other objects in the baskets to match each numeral.

- Make plastic bracelets or homemade bands of paper with a numeral on each to teach numerical ordering. Ask the child to place the bracelets on his arm in order from 1 through 10. You may have to begin with the bracelets on in the proper order, and then ask the child questions: "Which number comes first when you're counting? Can you find that number on one of the bracelets?" "Which number comes next?" "Which number comes after six?"

- Make pictures of cars with a numeral from 1 to 10 written on each, and ask the child to place the car pictures in numerical order. Extend this experience by asking, "How many cars are there altogether?" "How many cars are after 8?" "After 3?"

Bounce. On 9" × 12" cards, place different pictures, such as a house, two cars, three boys, four dogs, and so on, until there are 10 cards, with 10 objects on the last card. (Use stickers if desired.) The child is given instructions to bounce a ball once for every object on the card. Then the child is told to go various cards: "Go to the cars," or "Go to the house." The cards are placed around the room so the child must move about, bouncing the ball the number of times indicated by the number of objects on the cards. (Let him tap the ball if he cannot yet bounce it.)

> —*Variation #1:* Instead of pictures, draw shapes—a triangle, circle, square, or rectangle—on each card. Thus the game helps to strengthen recognition of the names of shapes as well as one-to-one correspondence.

— *Variation #2:* Place numerals from 1 to 10 around the room. Now show the child a card with objects on it, and ask him to find the numeral that tells how many objects are on the card.

- Number lines. Fold each of 10 sheets of heavy paper in half, and stand each up pup-tent fashion. Punch one hole in the first and write the numeral 1 below the hole. Punch two holes in the second and label it 2. Do the same for each sheet, from 3 through 10. Then instruct the child to fill the holes in each, in turn with golf tees, and place the folded sheets in numerical order. (Blocks of wood with holes drilled in them are also satisfactory.)
- Hammer 10 finishing nails into each of 10 pieces of wood 3" × 6".
- Line the 10 pieces of wood up and place a card with dots on it by each. The first card bears only one dot, the second, two dots, and so on, with the last bearing ten dots. (Numerals may be used when the child is able to identify them.) Let the child stretch an elastic band around the number of nails required to match the number of dots on the card by each piece.
- Prepare flannel shapes and flannel numerals so the child can match the correct number of shapes with each numeral.
- Write numerals on the sides or bottoms of the compartments in an egg carton. Tell the child to put the correct number of beans, buttons, or marshmallows, in each of the compartments.
- Make a number book by pasting the correct number of beans, pieces of macaroni, or colored squares next to the written numerals.
- Help the child set the table. Count the number of people who will be eating dinner and the number of plates, glasses, spoons, forks, and knives that will be needed.

COMPARISONS AND RELATIONSHIPS

- Observe and discuss objects and places in your environment, especially circles, squares, triangles, and rectangles.
- Put together jigsaw puzzles.
- While building with blocks, show the child a circle and let him find another circle. Do the same with other shapes.
- Provide shapes cut from colored construction paper. Allow the

child to make objects or designs by gluing them on other sheets of paper.

- Give the child many opportunities to sort objects, such as the laundry items, buttons, and shaped blocks. Egg cartons make excellent sorting trays for small items; muffin tins are good for larger items; and cottage-cheese cartons work well for still larger items.

- An assortment of odd-sized jars and lids gives the child an opportunity to match up lids with jars.

- Patterns. Arrange blocks, tiles, or squares of paper of two colors in various patterns (very simple ones at first). The child then duplicates the pattern you have made with the pieces. Also allow the child time to play freely with the materials. The child needs some time to get the feel of the exercise and explore its potentialities. When the child has learned to copy simple patterns, he is given a drawing of a pattern to follow.

    — *Variation #1:* Extending patterns. A pattern is extended by repeating the established pattern. For example, if you start a pattern of two reds, one white, two reds, and one white, the child should be able to then place colored pieces in the same sequence.

    — *Variation #2:* Hidden blocks. A pattern is started and extended far enough for the child to recognize it. Then a paper is placed over one or more of the blocks. The child concludes which blocks are covered by observing the pattern already established.

- *Bingo.* The child's bingo card, made of cardboard, shows objects in various quantities in each of its nine squares. For example, one square might show three apples, the next square, two birds, and so on. Master cards are held up one at a time for the child to see. The child covers his identical square with a bean or piece of paper, until he completes a combination of squares. There are many variations to this game. Numerals might be placed on the child's card and pictures or like numerals on the master cards. Be creative, but start with simple, concrete objects or pictures and work to symbolic images.

- Cut cardboard tubes, such as the rolls that waxed paper and toilet paper come on, into half-inch sections. Make sure you cut up rolls of different diameters. The object is for the child to experiment until he has arranged the pieces in the order of size. The same idea can be used with identical bottles filled with water in half-inch gradations.

COMBINING AND SEPARATING

Most preschool children do not benefit from anything more than a casual reference to combining and separating of objects. They are definitely not ready for formal addition and subtraction.

FRACTIONS

A child can begin to be aware of simple fractions and can extend his concept of wholeness.

- Provide for sharing in terms of half an apple, a whole cookie, or half a sandwich.
- Occasionally use half a sheet of paper in art projects.
- Use measuring spoons and cups in water and sand play and in preparation of food. Be sure to call the parts by their names: halves, thirds, and so forth.

MONEY

- Provide frequent opportunities to discuss with the child the value of coins and cost of toys or gifts.
- Identify the penny, nickel, dime, quarter, half-dollar, and dollar (silver and paper), in terms of their purposes.
- Provide materials especially play money, for a play store.
- Let the child pay for his own lunch, transportation, and candy.

MEASUREMENT

The preschool child of today will be caught in the conversion from the English system of measuring to the metric system. Activities in this section use the English system. However, if the parent desires, these could easily be converted to the metric system. It is recommended that you make comparisons only within each system such as feet with yards or centimeter with meter and do not make comparisons between the two systems.

- Ask the child questions about size and discuss various measuring instruments.
- Let the child play with a ruler and a yardstick. Ask them to measure and tell you how many yardsticks the bookcase or the couch is.
- Estimate how many small glasses are in a quart and how many cookies are in a box.
- Use many water-play and sand-play activities that call for weighing and measuring. (Use measuring cups and spoons.)
- Measure the distance a child runs or jumps or throws a ball.
- Post a large thermometer and call the child's attention to it. Check and record temperatures on the calendar periodically. Summarize your findings.
- Use the clock to determine actions. Call attention to the clock in relation to tasks.
- Show the child a bathroom scale. Let the child see what happens to the dial when weight is put on the scale. Weigh the child and other members of the family. Write the child's weight on a card so the child can see it written down. Show the child a heavy and light object. Invite the child to hold the objects. Talk about weight with the child. Discuss why some objects are heavier than others, although they may be smaller. Read labels specifying weights.
- Show the child a yardstick or measuring tape. Show him how long one inch is. Measure the child and tell him how many inches tall he is. Show him on the wall or the yardstick how tall he is. Write the child's height on a card so he can see the information written down and can show it to others.

appendixes

appendix a:
checklist for reading
readiness

PHYSICAL READINESS

Eyes

- Does the child seem comfortable in the use of his eyes (that is, does not squint, rub eyes, hold materials too close or too far from eyes?)
- Are the results of his eye screening test favorable?

Ears

- Is it apparent through his response to questions or directions that he is able to hear what is said?
- Does he respond to a low voice at 20 feet and a whisper at 15 feet?

Speech

- Does he articulate clearly?
- Does he speak in a group with some confidence?
- Does he speak without gross errors in pronunciation?
- Does he respond to suggestions for speech improvement?

From Manual for *Teaching the Reading-Readiness Program* of The Ginn Basic Readers, rev. ed., by David H. Russell and others, © copyright, 1957, 1953, 1948, by Ginn and Company (Xerox Corporation). Used with permission.

Hand-Eye Coordination

- Is he able to make his hands work together in cutting, using tools, or bouncing a ball?
- Can he perform simple tasks, such as stringing beads?

General Health

- Does he give an impression of good health?
- Does he seem well-nourished?
- Does a physical examination reveal good health?

MENTAL READINESS

Mind-set for Reading

- Does the child appear interested in books and reading?
- Does he ask the meanings of words or signs?
- Is he interested in the shapes of unusual words?

Mental Maturity

- Can he give reasons for his opinions about his own work or the work of others?
- Can he make or draw something to illustrate an idea as well as most children of his age?
- Is his memory span sufficient to allow memorization of a short poem or song?
- Can he tell a story without confusing the order of events?
- Can he listen or work for five minutes without restlessness?

Mental Habits

- Has the child established the habit of looking at a succession of items from left to right?
- Does his interpretation of pictures expand beyond mere enumeration of details?
- Does he grasp the fact that symbols may be associated with spoken language?
- Can he predict possible outcomes of a story?
- Can he remember the central thought of a story as well as the important details?
- Does he alter his own method to profit by another's example?

Language Patterns

- Does he take part in discussions and conversations?
- Is he effective in expressing his needs in group situations?
- Are the words used in the preprimers and primers part of his listening and speaking vocabulary?
- Does he listen to a story with evidence of enjoyment and is he able to recall parts of it?
- Does he listen to and understand the relationships inherent in such words as up and down, top and bottom, and big and little?
- Is he able to interpret an experience through dramatic play?

EMOTIONAL READINESS

Adjustment to Task

- Does the child see a task such as drawing, preparing for an activity, or cleaning up through to completion?
- Does he accept changes in family routine calmly?

- Does he appear to be happy and well-adjusted, as evidenced by a relaxed attitude, pride in work, and eagerness for a new task and activities?
- Does he follow adult leadership without showing resentment?

SOCIAL READINESS

Cooperation

- Does he work well with a group, taking his share of the responsibility?
- Does he cooperate in playing games with other children?
- Can he direct his attention to a specific learning situation?
- Does he listen rather than interrupt?

Sharing

- Does he share materials without monopolizing their use?
- Does he offer help when another person needs it?
- Does he await his turn in playing in games?
- Does he await his turn for help from adults?

Self-Reliance

- Does he work things through for himself without asking the adult about the next step?
- Does he take care of his clothing and materials?
- Does he find something to do when he finishes an assigned task?
- Does he take good care of materials assigned to him?

appendix b: books for a child

LISTENING BOOKS

Listen, Listen, ANN AND PAUL RAND, Harcourt Brace Jovanovich, Inc., 1970: All about the sounds you experience everyday but may not be aware of hearing.

The Listening Walk, PAUL SHOWERS, Crowell: A child walks with his father and hears many sounds. The reader listens also, 1961.

Too Much Noise, ANN MCGOVERN, Houghton Mifflin, 1967: Peter could not sleep because of the creaks and noises in his old house.

Why So Much Noise? retold by JANIAN DOMANSKA, Harper & Row, 1966: A mouse deer tricks a tiger and an old ape.

Do You Hear What I Hear? HELEN BORTEN, Abelard-Schuman, 1960.

The Country Noisy Book, MARGARET WISE BROWN, Harper & Row, 1940.

The Indoor Noisy Book, MARGARET WISE BROWN, Harper & Row, 1942.

The Noisy Book, MARGARET WISE BROWN, William R. Scott, 1939.

The Quiet Noisy Book, Harper & Row, 1950.

The Seashore Noisy Book, Harper & Row, 1941.

Shhh Bang, A Whispering Book, Harper & Row, 1943.

The Summer Noisy Book, Harper & Row, 1951.

The Winter Noisy Book, Harper & Row, 1947.

A Walk In The City, ROSEMARY AND RICHARD DAWSON, Viking Press, 1950.

All Sizes of Noises, KARLA KUSHKIN, Harper & Row, 1962.

The Little Fire Engine, LOIS LENSKI. Henry Z. Walck, Inc., 1946.

The Little Train, LOIS LENSKI. Henry Z. Walck, Inc., 1950.

ORAL-EXPRESSION BOOKS

Fight the Night, TOMIE DE PAOLA, J. B. Lippincott Company, 1968: Ronald decides to fight the night. He stays up all night but sleeps all the next day. Night laughs, "Ha, ha!" The child might relate his own experiences with the night. He could then share ideas about what he would do if he stayed up all night.

The Turnip, JANINA DOMANSKA, Macmillan, 1969: All the animals help pull up the large turnip. The child might make the sounds of the animals. He might create his own story using the basic idea.

Fortunately, REMY CHARLIP, Parents' Magazine Press, 1967: Tells of the fortunate and unfortunate events in Ned's life as he is on his way to a birthday party. A child might extend the story.

Rosie's Walk, PAT HUTCHINS, Macmillan, 1968: Tells of the problems a fox has while following a chicken who is taking a walk before dinner. The child might extend the story using his imagination.

READING-READINESS BOOKS

A for the Ark, ROGER DUVOISIN, Lothrop, 1952: The Old Testament story of the flood wherein Noah goes straight through the alphabet to be sure he gets two of every kind of animal.

Animals in the Zoo, FEODOR ROJAKOVKY, 1962: An animal alphabet book.

ABC, BRUNO MUNAIR, World, 1960: Imaginative, humorous, bolder colored.

ABC Bunny, WANDA GAG, Coward, 1933: A delightful ABC book giving a continuing story of a rabbit's adventures.

In a Pumpkin Shell, JOAN WALSH ANGLUND, Harcourt Brace Jovanovich, Inc., 1960: A Mother Goose ABC book with exquisite illustrations.

Inch by Inch, LEO LIONNI, Ivan Obolensky, 1960.

Over in the Meadow, JOHN LANGSTAFF, Harcourt, Brace Jovanovich, Inc., 1957.

LITERATURE BOOKS

Book of Nursery and Mother Goose Rhymes, compiled and illustrated by MARGUERITE DE ANGELI, Doubleday & Co., Inc., 1954.

The Golden Song Book, arranged by KATHERINE TAYLOR WESSEL, Golden Press, 1945.

Hi Diddle Diddle, A Book of Mother Goose Rhymes, (paperback), Scholastic Book Services, 1966.

Mother Goose, illustrated by TASHA TUDOR, Henry Z. Walck, Inc., 1944.

The Mother Goose Treasury, illustrated by RAYMOND BRIGGS, Coward, 1966.

A Cat Came Fiddling, and Other Rhymes of Childhood, PAUL KAPP, illustrated by IRENE HAAS, Harcourt Brace Jovanovich, Inc., 1956.

Ask Mr. Bear, MARJORIE FLACK, Macmillan, 1932.

Bedtime for Frances, RUSSELL HOBAN, Harper & Row, 1960.

The Big World and the Little House, RUTH KRAUSS, Harper & Row, 1949.

A Child's Good-Night Book, MARGARET WISE BROWN, Scott, 1950.

The Run Away Bunny, MARGARET WISE BROWN, 1952.

Goodnight Moon, Margaret Wise Brown, Harper & Row, 1947.

Little Auto, LOIS LENSKI, Henry Z. Walck, Inc., 1934.

The Little House, VIRGINIA LEE BURTON, Houghton Mifflin, 1942.

The Little House of Your Own, BEATRICE SCHENK DE REGNIERS, Harcourt Brace Jovanovich, Inc., 1954.

Little Toot, HARDIE GRAMATKY, G. P. Putnam's Sons, 1939.

Mike Mulligan and His Steam Shovel, VIRGINIA LEE BURTON, Houghton Mifflin, 1939.

Millions of Cats, WANDA GAG, Coward, 1923.

One Wide River to Cross, BARBARA EMBERLEY, Prentice-Hall, Inc., 1966.

Petunia, ROGER DUVOISIN, Knopf, 1950.

The Story about Ping, MARJORIE FLACK, Viking Press, 1933.

The Tale of Peter Rabbit, BEATRIX POTTER, Warne, 1903.

Goggles, EZRA JACK KEATS, Macmillan, 1969.

Debbie and Her Grandma, LOIS LENSKI, Henry Z. Walck, Inc., 1969.

Whose Mouse Are You? ROBERT KRAUS, Macmillan, 1970.

Brown Barnyard, DAHLOV IPCAR, Doubleday & Co., Inc., 1954.

Behind the Circus Tent, ALLAN JACOBS, Lerner, 1967.

Lovable Lyle, BERNARD WABER, Houghton Mifflin, 1969.

Little Tim and the Brave Sea Captain, EDWARD ARDIZZONE, Henry Z. Walck, Inc., 1936.

The Three Billy Goats Gruff, P. C. ASBJORNSEN, Doubleday & Co., Inc., 1943.

My Red Umbrella, ROBERT BRIGHT, Morrow, 1959.

Stone Soup, MARCIA BROWN, Scribner's Sons, 1947.

Nibble, Nibble, MARGARET W. BROWN, Scott, 1959.

Where's the Bunny? RUTH CARROLL, Henry Z. Walck, Inc., 1962.

A Pocketful of Cricket, REBECCA CAUDILL, Winston, 1964.

The Big Snow, BERTA HADEN, Macmillan, 1948.

Whistle For Willie, EZRA JACK KEATS, Viking, 1962.

Curious George, HANS A. REY, Houghton Mifflin, 1941.

Where the Wild Things Are, MAURICE SENDAK, Harper & Row, 1962.

And to Think I Saw It on Mulberry Street, DR. SEUSS, Vangaard, 1937.

Harry, the Dirty Dog, GENE ZION, Harper & Row, 1956.

The First Book of Poetry, selected by ISABELL J. PETERSON, Watts, 1954.

Favorite Poems Old and New, selected by HELEN FERRIS, Doubleday & Co., Inc., 1957.

The Wizard in the Well, HARRY BEHN, Harcourt Brace Jovanovich, Inc., 1956.

All Together, DOROTHY ALDIS, G. P. Putnam's Sons, 1952: Also *The Secret Place.*

Child's Garden of Verses, ROBERT L. STEVENSON, Grosset & Dunlap Inc., 1948.

My Poetry Book, compiled by JUNE PIERCE, Wonder Books, 1948.

Poems to Read to the Very Young, edited by JOSETTE FRANK, Random House, 1968.

CREATIVE-EXPRESSION BOOKS

May I Bring a Friend, BEATRICE SCHENK DE REGNIESS, Atheneum, 1967: A boy takes a different friend to the king's palace each day of the week. Draw a friend you might take.

Noodle, MUNRO LEAF, Four Winds Press, 1965: Noodle, a dog, can be any size and shape she desires with one wish. Ask the child to draw the size and shape he would like to be.

Birds of a Feather, WILLIE BAUM, Addison-Weslay, 1969: The story is told by pictures. The child might illustrate the story.

Drummer Hoff, BARBARA EMBERLY, Prentice-Hall, Inc., 1967: The illustrations show design and color. Observe with the child.

A Quangle, Wangles Hat, ED LEAR, Watts, 1970: The child might create his own hat. Draw a Quangle Wangle.

Do You Move as I Do? HELEN BORTEN, Abelard–Schuman, 1963: Stimulates the imagination and helps the child see many possibilities for movement.

Fredrick, LEO LIONNI, Random House, 1967: Excellent for role-playing.

Music through the Day, J. L. MURSELL, et al., Silver Burdett, 1956.

Music for Early Childhood, MARY J. NELSON, Silver Burdett, 1952.

Singing Day of Childhood, FLORENCE RAY, Denison, 1958.

Where the Wild Things Are, MAURICE SENDAK, Harper & Row, 1963.

SOCIAL-STUDIES BOOKS

A Friend Is Someone Who Likes You, JOAN ANGLUND, Harcourt Brace Jovanovich, Inc., 1958.

Choo Choo, VIRGINIA LEE BURTON, Houghton Mifflin, 1937.

Another Day, MARIE H. ETS, Viking Press, 1953.

Just Me, MARIE H. ETS, Viking Press, 1965.

All About Us, EVA K. EVANS, Capitol, 1947.

People Are Important, EVA K. EVANS, Capitol, 1957.

Growing Up, JEAN FRITZ, Rand McNally, 1951.

Is It Hard? Is It Easy? MARY M. GREEN, Young Scott Books, 1960.

Nobody Listens to Andrew, ELIZABETH GUILFOILE, Follett, 1957.

Just Like Everyone Else, KARLA KUSHIN, Harper & Row, 1959.

I Know a Lot of Things, ANN RAND, Harcourt Brace Jovanovich, Inc., 1956.

Timid Timothy, GWENEIVE WILLIAMS, Hale, 1940.

Youngest One, TARO YASHIMA, Viking Press, 1959.

Sam, ANN HERBERT SCOTT, McGraw-Hill, 1967.

Tommy's Big Problem, LILLU D. CHAFFIN, Lantern Press, 1965.

Too Many Crackers, HELEN BUCKLEY, 1966.

Peter's Chair, EZRA JACK KEATS, Harper & Row, 1967.

Grandfather and I, HELEN E. BUCKLEY, Lothrop, 1959.

Play with Me, MARIE HALL, Viking Press, 1955: Also *Just Me,* 1965.

Theodore Turtle, ELLEN MACGREGOR, McGraw-Hill, 1955.

House for Everyone, BETTY MILES, Knopf, 1958.

Laurie's New Brother, MIRIAM SCHLEIN, Abelard–Schuman, 1961.

Let's be Enemies, JANICE M. UNDRY, Harper & Row, 1961.

Papa Small, LOIS LENSKI, Henry Z. Walck, Inc., 1951.

Play with Me in the Forest, MARIE ETS. VIKING PRESS, 1955.

Daddies, What They Do All Day, HELEN W. PUNER, Lothrop, 1946.

SCIENCE BOOKS

Animals Of Farmer Jones and the Rooster Struts, RICHARD SCARRY, Golden Press, 1963.

Angus and the Cat and Angus and the Duck, MARJORIE FLACK, Doubleday & Co., Inc., 1930.

I Can Fly, RUTH KRAUSS, Golden Press, 1950.

Baby Farm Animals, GARTH WILLIAMS, Golden Press, 1959.

The Happy Owls, illustrated by CELESTINO PIATTI, Atheneum, 1963.

In the Forest, MARIE HALL ETS, Viking Press, 1944.

Animal Babies, TONI PALAZZO, Doubleday & Co., Inc., 1960.

A Tree Is Nice, JANICE UDRY, Harper & Row, 1956.

Make Way for Ducklings, Robert McCLOSKEY, Viking Press, 1941.

Swimmy, LEO LIONI, Pantheon, 1963.

Where Have You Been? MARGARET WISE BROWN, Hastings, 1952.

Did A Bear Just Walk There? ANN RAND, Harcourt Brace, Jovanovich, Inc., 1966.

The Hungry Book, CHARLOTTE STEINER, Knopf, 1967.

Animals Should Definitely Not Wear Clothing, JUDI BARRETT, McCleveland, 1970.

The Old Barn, CAROL CARRICK, Merrill, 1966.

Fox and the Fire, MISKA MILES, Brown, 1966.

All Aboard the Train and the Big Red Bus, ETHEL KESSLER, Doubleday & Co., Inc., 1964.

The Big Book of Fire Engines, GEORGE J. ZAFFO, Grosset & Dunlap, Inc., 1958.

The Big Book of Real Boats and Ships, GEORGE J. ZAFFO, Grosset & Dunlap, Inc., 1959.

The Big Book of Real Building and Wrecking Machines, GEORGE J. ZAFFO, Grosset & Dunlap, Inc., 1951.

The Big Book of Real Trains, GEORGE J. ZAFFO, Grosset & Dunlap Inc., 1953.

The Big Book of Real Trucks, GEORGE J. ZAFFO, Grosset & Dunlap Inc., 1958.

Red Light, Green Light, GOLDEN MACDONALD, Doubleday & Co., Inc., 1944.

The Plant Sitter, GENE ZION, Harper & Row, 1959. Also *All Fall Down,* 1951.

The Carrot Seed, RUTH KRAUSS, Harper & Row, 1945.

The Sunshine Book, HELEN FEDERICO, Golden Press, 1964.

White Snow, Bright Snow, ALVIN TRESSELT, Lothrop, 1947.

MATHEMATICS BOOKS

Ten Little Foxhounds, GIFFORD AMBLER, Grosset & Dunlap Inc., 1958.

Brown Cow Farm, DAHLOV IPEAR, Doubleday & Co., Inc., 1959.

Seven Chicks Missing, KATHERINE BARR, Henry Z. Walck, Inc., 1962.

One Bright Monday Morning, ARLINE BARUM, Random House, 1962.

All Kinds of Time, HARRY BEHN, Harcourt Brace Jovanovich, Inc., 1959.

The Smallest Boy in the Class, JERROLD BEIM, Morrow, 1959.

All Around You, JEANNE BENDICK, McGraw-Hill, 1951.

Big and Little, Up and Down, Early Concepts of Size and Direction, ETHEL S. BERKLEY, Scott, 1960.

The Five Chinese Brothers, CLAIRE BISHOP, Hale, 1958.

A Cat Can't Count, BLOSSOM BUDLEY, Lothrop, 1962.

Poems for Counting, ALICE B. CAMPBELL, Holt, Rinehart and Winston, 1963.

Numbers, HELEN FEDENICO, Golden Press, 1963.

Chicken Little, Count to Ten, MARGARET FRISKEY, Grosset & Dunlap, Inc., 1946.

Let's Do Fingerplays, MARION GRAYSON, Robert Luce, 1962.

One, Two, Buckle My Shoe, GAIL HALEY, Doubleday & Co., Inc., 1961.

Heavy is a Hippopotamus, MIRIAM SCHLIEN, Scott, 1954.

appendix c:
resources for parents

LISTENING RESOURCES

ADAMS, HARLEM M. "Learning to be Discriminating Listeners," *The English Journal*, 36:11–15, 1947.

DAWSON, MILDRED. *Learning to Listen*, Language Arts Notes, No. 3 (Yonkers-on-Hudson, N.Y.: World Book), p. 1.

NICHOLS, RALPH G. *Are You Listening?* New York: McGraw-Hill, 1954.

ORAL-EXPRESSION RESOURCES

AKIN, JOHNNYE. *And So We Speak*. Englewood Cliffs, N.J.: Prentice-Hall, Inc., 1958.

GETZEL, J. W., et al. "Giftedness and Creativity," *Newsletter* (Chicago: University of Chicago, November 1960).

LONG, CHARLES. *Will Your Child Learn to Talk Correctly?* Albuquerque, N.M.: The New Mexico Publishing Co., 1957.

WARD, WINIFRED. *Playmaking with Children*, (2nd ed.), New York: Appleton-Century-Crofts, 1957.

READING RESOURCES

DURKIN, DOLORES. "Should the Very Young be Taught to Read?" *Nea J.*, 52:3, 1963, pp. 20–23.

GETZELS, J. W., AND P. W. JACKSON. *Creativity and Intelligence*. New York: John Wiley & Sons, 1962.

HYMES, JAMES L., JR., *Before the Child Reads.* New York: Row, Peterson, 1958.

MACDONALD, J. B., AND R. R. LEEPER (eds.), *Language and Meaning.* Washington, D.C.: ASCD, 1966.

SHELDON, W. D.   "Should the Very Young Be Taught to Read?" *Nea J.*, 52:3, 1963, pp. 58-64.

WRITING RESOURCES

HERRICK, V. E.   "Manuscript and Cursive Writing," *Childhood Education,* 37:6, 1961, pp. 264-276.

McINTOSH, HELEN K., AND WILHELMINA HILL.   *How Children Learn to Write,* Bulletin No. 2. Washington, D.C.: U.S. Office of Education, 1953.

ART RESOURCES

BLAND, JANCE C.   *Art of the Young Child,* New York: Museum of Modern Art, 1957.

GATES, G. F.   "Why Children's Art?" *Child. Educ.,* 41:3, 1964, pp. 133-134.

HOOVER, LOUIS F.   *Art Activities for the Very Young.* Worcester, Mass.: Davis Publishing Inc., 1963.

LINDSTROM, MIRIAM.   *Children's Art.* Berkeley, Calif.: University of California Press, 1957.

MUSIC RESOURCES

Song and Music Books

BAILEY, CHARITY (ed.).   *Sing a Song,* Plymouth Music Co., New York.

BERTIAL, INEZ (ed.). *Complete Nursery Song Book,* Lothrop, New York.

COLEMAN, SATIS N., AND ALICE G. THORN. *Singing Time,* John Day Co., New York.

Cooperative Recreation Services, Inc. (Delaware, Ohio). *Pocket Songs:* Small booklet containing hundreds of folk tunes from around the world.

LANDECK, BEATRICE (ed.). *Songs to Grow On.* Edward Marks Music Publishers-William Sloane, New York.

MILLER, MARY AND PAULA ZAJAN (collectors). *Finger Plays.* G. Schirmer, New York.

NELSON, MARY J. *Music in Early Childhood.* Morristown, N.J.: Silver Burdett, 1952.

Children's Records

Activity Songs for Kids, MARCIA BERMAN, Folkways FC 7023.

American Game and Activity Songs, PETE SEEGER, Folkways, FC 7002.

Children's Concert, OSCAR BRAND, Wonderland, 1438.

Counting Games and Rhythms for Little Ones, ELLA JENKINS, Folkways FC 7056.

Ding-Dong School Singing Games, MITCH MILLER, Golden GLP 49.

March Along, Wonderland 1486.

More Songs to Grow On, ALAN MILLS, Folkways, FC 7009.

Peter and the Wolf Young Person's Guide To The Orchestra Vox, PL 9280.

Recordings For Children. New York Library Association, Children's and Young Adults' Service Section, 20 W. 53rd St., New York, N.Y.

Sing a Song of Childhood, MARJORIE BENNETT, Wonderland, 3028.

Song And Play Time With Pete Seeger, PETE SEEGER, Folkways, FC 7526.

Songs to Grow On, WOODY GUTHRIE, Folkways FC 7005.

Train to the Zoo, Children's Record Guild 1001.

Winnie the Pooh, JACK GILFORD, Golden LP 95.

RHYTHM AND DANCE RESOURCES

ANDREWS, GLADYS. Creative Rhythmic Movement for Children. Englewood Cliffs, N.J.: Prentice-Hall, Inc., 1954.

EMERSON, NORA B. *Rainbow Rhythms.* Atlanta: Emory University, 1952.

HARVEY, SISTER ANN. *Rhythms and Dances for Preschool and Kindergarten.* New York: G. Schirmer, Inc., #40734.

KUHN, JACQUELINE. *33 Rhythms for Children.* New York: Bregman Vocco and Conn, Inc., 1956.

MASON, B. *Drums, Tom-toms and Rattles.* New York: A. S. Barnes, 1938.

STAPES, R. "Fun with Rhythm Instruments," *Musical Fun Books.* Chicago: Follett, 1955.

WATERMAN, ELIZABETH. *Rhythm Book.* New York: A. S. Barnes, 1936.

PLAY RESOURCES

AARON, D., AND BONNIE P. WINAWER. *Child's Play, A Creative Approach to Playspaces for Today's Children.* New York: Harper & Row, 1965.

BAKER, BATHERINE READ. *Let's Play Outdoors.* Washington, D.C.: NAEYC, 1966.

BURNS, SYLVIA E. "Children Respond to Improvised Equipment,"
Young Children, 20:1 (1964), pp. 23-33.

MATTERSON, E. M. *Play and Playthings for the Preschool Child.*
Baltimore: Penguin Books, 1963.

NICHOLAYSEN, MARY. "Dominion in Children's Play: Its Meaning
and Management," *Young Children,* 22:1 (1966) pp. 20-29.

Play—Children's Business: Guide to Selection of Toys and Games,
7-A. Washington, D.C.: ACEI, 1963.

SOCIAL-STUDIES RESOURCES

FOSHAY, ARTHUR W., et al. *Children's Social Values.* New York:
Bureau of Publications, Teachers College, Columbia University, 1954.

HORWICH, FRANCES. "Orienting the Threes and Fours," *Childhood
Education,* 26:10-13, September 1949.

RUDOLPH, MARGUERITE. *Living and Learning in Nursery School.*
New York: Harper & Row, 1954.

WILCOCKSON, MARY. *Social Education of Young Children.* Washington, D.C.,: National Education Association, 1950.

SCIENCE RESOURCES

BLOUGH, GLENN, AND ALLAN L. DODD. "Children Are Their Own
Resources," *Childhood Education,* 34:21, September 1957.

FREEMAN, KENNETH, et al. *Helping Children Understand Science.*
Philadelphia: John C. Winston, 1954.

HELFRICH, JOHN E. "Science Experiences and Kindergarten
Children," *Science and Children,* 1:6 (1964), pp. 1-28.

HUBLER, CLARK, *Working with Children in Science.* Boston:
Houghton Mifflin, 1956.

STANT, MARGARET A.　"Let's Enrich the Science Experiences," *Lets Try This in Nursery School and Kindergarten,* College Park, Md.: Sanmar Pub., 1963, pp. 7–16.

MATHEMATICS RESOURCES

ANDREWS, F. E.　*Numbers Please.* Boston: Little, Brown & Company, 1961.

MARKS, J. L., C. R. PURDY, AND L. B. KINNEY.　*Teaching Arithmetic for Understanding.* New York: McGraw-Hill, 1964.

PIAGET, J. et al.　*The Child's Conception of Numbers.* New York: Humanities Press, Inc., 1952.

SWENSON, ESTHER S.　*Teaching Arithmetic to Children.* New York: Macmillan, 1964.

appendix d:
bibliography

BLOOM, BENJAMIN S., *Stability and Change in Human Characteristics*, New York: John Wiley & Sons, Inc.,1964.

CALDWELL, BETTYE M., "What Is the Optimal Learning Environment For the Young Child?" *American Journal of Orthopsychiatry*, XXXVIII (January, 1967).

CHERRY, CLARE, Creative Movement for the Developing Child: A *Nursery School Handbook for Non-Musicians* (rev. ed.) Palo Alto, California: Fearon Publishers, Inc., 1971.

CHAPMAN, JUNE, a collection of unpublished games, mimeographed.

ELKIND, DAVID. "The Development of Quantitative Thinking: A Systematic Replication of Piaget's Studies," *Journal of Genetic Psychology*, 98, 1961.

GORDON, IRA, speech delivered at the conference on The Young Child: Florida's Future, at the University of Florida, June 16, 1967.

HESS, ROBERT D., "Inventory of Compensatory Education Projects," Chicago, Ill.: School of Education, University of Chicago, mimeographed, 1965.

HILDEBRAND, V., *Introduction to Early Childhood Education*, pp. 3-27, New York: Macmillan, 1971.

HOLT, JOHN, *How Children Learn*, foreward, New York: Pitman, 1967.

HONSTEAD, CAROLE, "The Development Theory of Jean Piaget" (paper), Oregon State University: 1968.

LEEPER, S. H., DALES, R. J., SKIPPER, D. S., AND WITHERSPOON, R. L., *Good Schools for Young Children: A Guide for Working with Three, Four and Five Year Old Children,* New York: Macmillan, 1968.

LOGAN, LILLIAN M., *Teaching the Young Child: Methods of Pre-school and Primary Education,* Boston: Houghton Mifflin, 1960.

MILNER, ESTHER, "A Study of the Relationship Between Reading Readiness in Grade One School Children and Patterns of Parent-Child Interactions," *Child Development,* 22, 1951.

PORTER, PARA, *Practical Ideas and Activities for Pre-School Enrichment Program,* Wolfe City, Texas: Henington Publishing Co. 1966.

READ K., *The Nursery School: A Human Relationships Laboratory,* (4th ed.), Philadelphia: W. B. Saunders, Company, 1966.

SCARFE, N. B., "Play is Education," in *Readings from Childhood Education,* Washington, D. C., ACEI, 1966.

TARNEY, E. D., *What Does the Nursery School Teach?* (rev. ed.), p. 71, Washington D.C.: NAEYC, 106, 1965.

TAYLOR, BARBARA J., *A Child Goes Forth* (revised ed.) Ch. 1-9, Provo, Utah: Brigham Young University Press, 1975.

TODD, V. E. AND HEFFERNAN, H. *The Years Before School: Guiding Preschool Children* (2nd ed.), New York: Macmillan, 1970.

UZGIRIS, INA C., "Situational Generality of Conservation, *Child Development,* 35, 1964.

WINN, MARIE, AND PORCHER, MARY ANN, *The Play Group Book,* New York: Macmillan, 1967.

index